Korean Impact on Japanese Culture
Japan's Hidden History

Korean Impact
Japan's

on Japanese Culture
Hidden History

by Dr. Jon Carter Covell & Alan Covell

HOLLYM

Copyright © 1984
by Dr. Jon Carter Covell & Alan Covell

All rights reserved

First published in 1984
Second printing, 1986
Third printing, 1987
Fourth printing, 1990
by Hollym International Corp.
18 Donald Place
Elizabeth, New Jersey 07208 U.S.A.

Published simultaneously in Korea
by Hollym Corporation; Publishers
14-5 Kwanchol-dong, Chongno-gu
Seoul 110-111 Korea
Phone:(02)735-7554 Fax:(02)730-5149

ISBN: 0-930878-34-5
Library of Congress Catalog Card Number: 83-81484

Printed in Korea

DEDICATION

This book is dedicated to the multitudes in Japan, Korea and the rest of the world who have yet to realize the central position of Korea in Japan's early history and her cultural development.

Dr. Jon Carter Covell and Alan Covell
   1,515 th year (1984) of the "Horseriders" coming to Japan.

CONTENTS

PREFACE   6

INTRODUCTION: HORSERIDING NOMADS   8

Part I The "Horseriders" Arrive: Japan's Pre-History

1 *The Land of Across*   12
Southward Flight of a Princess 12/Jingu's "Arranged Marriage" 12/ Jingu and "Valiant Old Bear" (Takechiuchi) 15/Death and Prophecy 15/ Subjugation of Kaya (Silla) 17/The Invasion of Japan 18/The "Love Child" and His Conception 20/Battles and Deceit 21/Jingu Received "Seven-Branched Sword" from Paekche 22/"Seven Little One Mirror" from Paekche 23/Inscription of 48 Characters 23/Mythological Scenes 24

2 *Ojin: Friend of Paekche*   25
Jingu's Son, Ojin, Consolidates Power 25/Ojin and Trial by Ordeal 25/ Paekche's Gifts to Ojin 25/Chinese Letters Arrive from Paekche 26/Ojin Popularized as Shinto's "God of War" 26/Cultural Dependence upon Korea 27/Women as Special Gifts 27/Shamanist Beliefs and Horserider Tombs 28/Tomb of Ojin 30

3 *Nintoku: Divine Despot*   32
Nintoku and Contest for the Throne 32/Palace Architecture 32/Marriage to the "Rock Princess" 33/Falconing Comes from Paekche to Osaka 34/ Nintoku's "Great Tomb" 35/Archeology Officially Discouraged 36/ Scholarly Pursuits Begin Displacing Martial Arts 36

4 *Puyo's Rock Deity*   38
Later Horserider Rulers 38/Japan's Capital Moved to Shrine of the Puyo Rock Diety 40/Rocks as a Sign of Puyo Legitimacy 40/Puyo Rock Deity Shrine Decreases in Importance 41/Muretsu the Mad: A Literary Device? 42

Part II Koreans and Japan's Historic Period

1 Asuka and Early Buddhism — 44
Asuka: An Early Settlement for Korean Immigrants 44/Soga's "Marriage Politics" 44/Paekche's Introduction of Buddhism 44/Buddhism Foments Internal Jealousies 45/Paekche's Continuing Cultural Input 46/Buddhism Used to Woo Japan's Court 46/Soga Umako Speeds the Importation of Buddhist Influence 47/Shintoist Backlash and the Burning of Temples 48/Victory of the Soga Forces and the Ascendance of Buddhism 48/Soga Umako Builds Hoko-ji 48/Hoko-ji Meant Wholesale Importation from Paekche 49/"Horse's Child" Soga Takes over Supreme Rule (592 A.D.) 50

2 Shotoku Taishi, "The Father of Japanese Buddhism" — 52
Shotoku and Buddhist Culture 52/Shotoku's Favorite Temple: Horyu-ji 53/Master Builders from Paekche 53/Horyu-ji Pagoda: Paekche Masterpiece 54/Korean Nobility 56/Paekche Kuanyin, called "Kudara Kannon" in Japan 57/The "Dream Hall" Kuanyin (Yumedono Kannon) 62/Tamamushi Shrine: Jewel of Asuka Art 70/Horyu-ji's Bronze Triad 76/Canopies for the Buddha: The Vault of Heaven 82/The Four Heavenly Kings 84/A Tapestry of Paradise 87/Koryu-ji's Maitreya: Testimonial to Shotoku Taishi 89

3 Korean Impact on Japan's Nara Epoch — 90
Gyogi 90/Nara's Giant Statue — Korean Success? 90/Korean Magicians and Holy Monks 93/Unofficial Transmissions of Culture 94

4 Korean Influence on Later Japanese Art — 96
Korean Influence on the "Japanese Only" Epoch 96/Impact of Official Missions on Culture 97/Korean Input into Japan's 15th Century Ink Painting 99/Korean Tigers in Momoyama Japan 102/Korean Ceramics and Cultural Invasion 105/Twentieth Century Impact on Japanese Folk Art Movement 109

APPENDIX — 110

ABRIDGED BIBLIOGRAPHY — 113

Dust Cover (Front): Two sculptural representations of Maitreya, the Buddha-of-the-Future, meditating in Tusita Heaven. The left-hand statue is of gilt bronze and owned by the National Museum, Seoul. The right-hand Maitreya is among the most famous and admired Buddhist statues in Japan. It has been owned by Koryu-ji, a Kyoto temple, for over thirteen and a half centuries. The authors contend that both are creations of Korean artists; one ended up in a temple built for Korean textile workers, seventh-century residents in an area later to become Kyoto. It is unusual to have two such similar works of art, since most Korean originals of early days perished through warfare. Over the centuries Japan became a vast Korean Art Museum. UNESCO estimates over 100,000 artifacts of Korea now preserved in Japan.

Dust Cover (Rear): A mural painting discovered on the walls of a Kyushu tomb. This depicts the arrival of men and horses, by boat with a heavenly (flying) horse at the top, since the "Horseriders" who came to Japan in 369 A.D. were deep believers in Shamanist magic. The official court histories covered up this major event, and had Empress Jingu conquer Korea, instead of coming from Korea to conquer Japan.

Front Endpaper: Aerial view of the mounded tomb assigned to "Emperor Nintoku," second in the imperial line of "Horserider" rulers. The Imperial Household Agency forbids its archeological excavation, but a storm in 1872 uncovered many Korean artifacts buried here.

Rear Endpaper: On the left is a famous Korean portrayal of a tiger. On the right is one of many tiger paintings against gold leaf backgrounds, which were created in Japan after Hideyoshi's troops invaded Korea. "Tigermania" swept the country and influenced its art. Here is a tiger with a leopard. Obviously the artist is working from a skin, as both animals were prevalent in Korea, but not native to Japan.

First Titlepage: Gilt-bronze stirrups from proto-historic Japan. The intricacy of design and polished metal-working technique evidenced here were beyond the grasp of native Japanese smiths during this time period.

Titlepage: One mural from a Fukuoka Prefecture tomb, which depicts the landing of the "traditional" first emperor, Jimmu Tenno. Although the Nihongi states that a heavenly crow led Jimmu to Ise, this painting's presence in Kyushu points the direction to the real founders and their landing site.

Preface: Tiger hunting scene from Momoyama-period Japan, when things Korean and tigers were in high fashion among artists.

NOTES ON ROMANIZATION

The Romanization of Korean words in this book follows the McCune-Reischauer system, but omits the diacrtical marks indicating vowel shifts and aspirations. Romanization of Japanese words follows the Hepburn system. Chinese words are romanized using the Wade-Giles system, also omitting diacritical marks. All foreign words are usually italicized in the first usage, and in standard type thereafter. Book titles are italicized in every case. Japanese names are written with the family name first.

PREFACE

Each nation recognizes a few places of major importance to its early history; for example, the U.S.A. points to Plymouth Rock, Jamestown and Saint Augustine as famous spots where immigrants landed when the country was still in its infancy; in like fashion, Japan has three places crucial to her beginnings: Izumo Shrine, Ise Shrine, and Iso-no-Kami. However, these are not just places for sightseeing. Rather, they exude an air of holiness, fed by the traditions of State Shinto.

Millions of Japanese perform a pilgrimage to Ise Shrine, home of the Sun Goddess, each year, just as Moslems try to journey to Mecca, their holy city, at least once in a lifetime. Those who reach Mecca march so many times around the Black Rock of the central Kaaba, survival of Arabia's early days of animistic worship.

Those who reach Ise Shrine, bow before thick curtains which screen from their view a wooden building which is purported to hold an ancient mirror, sacred to the Sun Goddess, progenitor of the present line of rulers, according to Japan's oldest history books (712 and 720 A.D.).

Somewhat less frequently visited is Izumo Shrine, first raised by an important colony of Korean immigrants, founded over 2,000 years ago. Its Shinto Shrine is sacred to the immigrants' patron deity, the Storm God, Susa-no-oo, admittedly the "older brother of the Sun Goddess" in the Shinto pantheon of nature deities.

Third in importance among Shinto shrines connected with Japan's very early history is Iso-no-Kami Jingu, or "The Shrine of the Puyo Rock Deity." This is located on a wooded slope, a twenty-minute walk from the railroad station in the heart of Asuka, homeland of Japan's earliest attempts at "culture" under a somewhat centralized government. Advanced civilization and technology were brought to the islands by a group of cavalry, embarked on boats, led by a redoubtable princess from the Puyo tribe's "divine heritage."

Most Japanese feel it their patriotic duty to journey to Ise at least once, and many have heard that the "sacred mirror of the Sun Goddess" is supposedly kept there, to be seen only by the eyes of the reigning emperor, her descendant.

Japan's well-educated realize that Izumo Shrine is much older than Ise and thus establishes the fact that the first large groups of immigrant-settlers with knowledge beyond the Stone Age, came from Korea, particularly Silla.

Iso-no-Kami is well-known to Japan's ancient history buffs. (It is less frequently visited by the populace-at-large than Ise.) The "sacred sword" within this Shinto shrine is not the fabled one drawn from the tail of a dragon by the Storm God Susa, nor the one allegedly given by the Sun Goddess to her descendant (Jimmu) to use "in conquering the land (of Japan)." It is, instead, a very real iron sword, with a Shamanistic shape. This artifact verifies the actual "conquest of Japan." It is inscribed with Chinese characters of gold which include a date corresponding to 369 A.D.

In that year few living on the Japanese islands could read Chinese and only the most educated elite in the Paekche Kingdom knew Chinese (then East Asia's only written language). However, this sword authenticates the conquest of Japan in 369 A.D. by a group, herein termed "The Horseriders," led by a beautiful young princess from Puyo named Jingu.

In their attempt at a later date to cover up this successful invasion by alien horseriders, the earliest Japanese written histories (eighth century) pictured Jingu as conquering all of Korea. Too dramatic and memorable a figure to totally pass over, the dynamic Jingu was converted into a purely Japanese queen and her "invasion" twisted around 180 degrees.

Perhaps not one percent of today's Japanese realize the significance of the unusually shaped iron artifact lying hidden behind curtains at Iso-no-Kami, have heard of the Puyo tribe, or know that this was Puyo rulers' holy of holies, their animistic shrine to the magic of rocks. Few have heard that Ise's "sacred mirror" was lost long ago, or even conceive of some details contained in this book.

The initial impetus for this volume came more than four decades ago, while researching at Columbia University. Facts or bits of information have kept thrusting themselves into view since that time, whether living in Kyoto, Japan, in Hawaii, or more recently in Seoul, Korea. Finally the sum total added up to so much that at least the tip of the iceberg demanded to be printed — to pull back the curtains covering up the tremendous importance of Korea and Koreans upon Japan's development, particularly its artistic culture, for more than 1,500 years.

INTRODUCTION: HORSERIDING NOMADS

Throughout Central and Northern Asia the horseback nomad became a potent force for historical change not to be reckoned with on a time-table. These peoples, whose largest unit might be a group of tribes banded together by a charismatic leader in their search for better pastures, sometimes overturned corrupt dynasties in China or India or swept southward into the Manchurian plains from the sub-arctic regions of Siberia. They burned fixed fortifications, carried off slaves of both sexes, as well as other loot that could be packed into their always traveling caravans. The Hindu Kush mountains or China's "Great Wall" failed to stop them.

The more famous of these nomadic empires usually lasted for only a brief span of history, bequeathing to Western researchers such names as Kanishka, Attila the Hun, Ghengis Khan, Tamerlane and Babur the Tiger. Tribes of nomads such as the Scythians, Huns, Tartars, Turks, Mongols and Manchus are remembered mostly for their conquests. The horsemen of the unforgiving steppes of Asia met and subdued the town-dwellers of China, India and Europe.

About the time of the Christian era, the southern part of what is now termed "Korea"(a line of demarcation which would roughly fit the 38th Parallel), was occupied by agriculturalists, or hunter-gatherers and fishermen in small tribal groups, holding loose alliances with other tribes, some of which were linked in maritime trade with Japan across the Straits of Tsushima. Nothing like a coherent monarchy had yet emerged; distances and rugged terrain isolated certain tribal federations from others, beginning the boundaries of what were to later become the three kingdoms of Korea along geographic lines.

Above the line which now bisects the peninsula, Altai-speaking horseback nomads fought among themselves and their wild cousins for territory and domination. The Chinese Han dynasty at one time controlled a small area in the Taedong River Basin called Lolang (Nangnang in Korean). It had contact with these intractable horseback warriors who conquered all less-advanced cultures with double-curved bows, cavalry tactics, and sheer berserker ferocity.

The Chinese protectorate of Nangnang passed into the hands of Koguryo during the fourth century, thus separating the Han Chinese from what was their last "colony" in the peninsula proper. At this time, Koguryo, as records indicate, was a splinter group of the Northern Puyo. It had become the fastest-rising star among the horseback tribes on the Korean peninsula. Koguryo cut off the areas where the Northern Puyo would have expanded southward and drove a group now known only as "Eastern Puyo" to "the shore of the Eastern Sea." These Eastern Puyo, cut off from their northern kinsmen, moved southward along Korea's coast until they combined with less-advanced tribes to form the basis for what was to later become Kaya and Silla kingdoms.

The original kingdom of Puyo is said by legend to have been founded by the son of a Heavenly King; its rulers were shaman-priests, responsible for whatever befell the tribe. Holding to their rich grassland area between the Sungari and Yalu Rivers in Manchuria, the Northern Puyo had seen and weathered nomadic invasions and crippling internal rebellions by the time the Hsien-pi came pouring out of the Manchurian forest in the early fourth century. The Han Chinese empire had fallen into disarray, and could no longer help "the most civilized of the Eastern Barbarians," as the Puyo had been termed.

All this activity led to the destruction of the Northern Puyo state, and an eventual migration southward into the Korean peninsula of some of its elements. The oldest existing records mentioning this Volkerwanderungen were not written until four hundred years later; that story was fragmentarily compiled (in Japan) by descendants who were by then a world apart in temperament from their nomadic ancestors.

The Puyo Horseriders, with their iron swords and armor, who would be harangued by their shamans before going into battle, might easily have fit into the stories of *Conan, the Barbarian*. This Puyo migration in search of greener pastures set the stage for the separation of Korea into three, distinct martial kingdoms and also for the subsequent conquest of Japan's Yamato Plain by the Puyo, "Children of the Rock."

Part I Titlepage: This gilt-bronze crown is one of the very few extant from Horserider-period Paekche. Kwangju National Museum.

PART I

THE "HORSERIDERS" ARRIVE: JAPAN'S PRE-HISTORY

1 THE LAND OF ACROSS

Southward Flight of a Princess

In 346 A.D. a small, weary group of once-proud Puyo tribesmen had moved southward towards the Korean peninsula after the Hsien-bi left their capital a smoking ruins. This van of loyal nobles who had not been captured by the enemy protected a baby princess, the last of the pure Puyo ruling line. On their way south, the group picked up disaffected mercenaries who had served the rulers of Lolang (Pyongyang area today).

A group of what may have begun as only a few hundred, including women and children, formed a train stretching southwards towards Paekche, which had itself been founded by former refugees from the north. The infant princess served as a sort of bargaining chip; her presence lent continued life to aspirations for further conquests in virgin territory.

The Puyo nomads were much more militant than those then inhabiting the southern part of the Korean peninsula (largely farmers and fishermen). Horsemen of Puyo could both eat and drink in the saddle and even sleep there by stretching across the horse's neck. The double-curved bow, shot from a horse's back, was their weapon in a "Fight, Win or Die" encounter.

The tradition for the founding of Korea's Paekche Kingdom relates that "Paek," which means "100," refers to the number of followers that the progenitors brought with them from the more northern kingdom of Koguryo. A small band of horseriding nomads could easily subdue much larger numbers of sedentary settlers.

Kunchogo, who ruled over Paekche from 346 to 375 A.D., no doubt awaited with misgiving when he heard of the refugees from northern Puyo. Either they would become loyal retainers assisting his further conquests,

One section from a twenty-foot-long procession with 250 figures. The painted troops wear various kinds of iron and bronze armor. This mural is dated mid-4th century, and is located in North Korea. (Anak Tomb #3, 357 A.D., Hwanghae Province)

or he would be faced with hardened Puyo warriors, who had battled their way through 1,000 miles of turmoil to reach his southern territory. The infant princess might be descended in theory from Haeburu, "The King of Heaven," but Paekche also claimed the same line. Fratricide was frequent among the Puyo, but perhaps a female rival need not be killed. She could be profitably employed in the game of marriage politics.

Jingu's "Arranged Marriage"

Upon arrival at the Paekche court, the ref-

This haniwa warrior, now in the Arikawa Archeological Museum, wears the same type of armor as seen in the North Korean painted tomb.

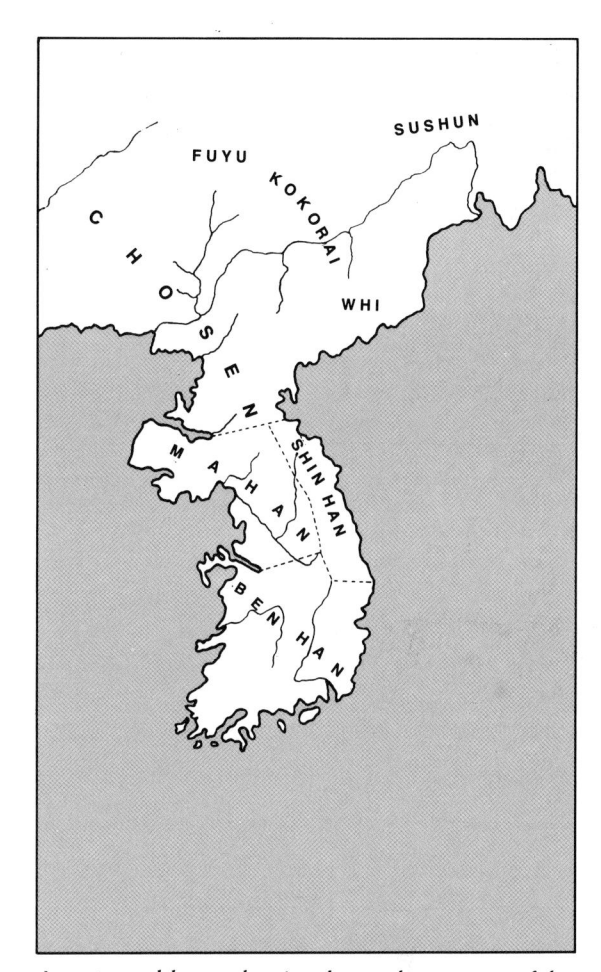

A century-old map showing the northern extent of the Puyo (Fuyu) kingdom, and its offshoot, Koguryo. (From Griffis' History of Corea)

ugee Puyo lacked a leader. The infant, although a princess of the Shamanist line, could not yet "communicate with the gods" (had not yet experienced *shinbyong* or "shaman sickness") and was too young to lead men to war. It appears that most of the Puyo refugees joined the Paekche king in his further conquests of the Ma Han people.

By the time the princess reached maturity, the Paekche king had other strategy on his mind than just retaining this girl of the direct bloodline in his retinue. The jealous queen could realize that this princess, if she had a child, it would hold as good a claim to the throne as her own. To the east of expanding Paekche lay the long-established Kaya League, rulers of city-states, who also claimed descent from the "King of Heaven." In the mid-fourth century the Kaya League was ruled by King Chuai. By having young Jingu marry this Chuai, a peaceful alliance of Paekche and Kaya might be developed.

All records agree that King Chuai was older than Jingu; he already had two grown sons in line for his throne. The princess Jingu was no doubt intended as a pleasing diver-

above
A modern Korean shaman performing. Although Seoul shamans continue the ecstatic tradition of Scythian-Altai-Siberian groups, it is notably different in that women play a larger part than men.
above right
Japanese female shaman, called a miko. Her performances are usually less frenzied than those of a Korean mudang.
below right
Chest armor of a foot soldier, excavated in the Kaya region. Kyemyong University Museum, Taegu.
opposite page
Haniwa wearing Kaya armor. Kyoto Univ. Museum.

sion for his declining years, when she became one of the consorts at his court (located at Koryong, modern Taegu).

Meanwhile, Jingu had suffered the traditional "shaman sickness" and was now enabled to become a mouthpiece of the Shamanist deities. From now on, Jingu could speak with the authority of the gods, foretelling future triumphs or tragedies for the royal house.

Jingu and "Valiant Old Bear" (Takechiuchi)

When Jingu arrived at Chuai's court, she may not have been too pleased. Her elderly husband surveyed a loosely-bound trading empire which apparently included the island of Tsushima, the northern coast of Kyushu Island, and a shipping network which stretched from what is now Pusan to present-day Taegu, along the Naktong River which connected the two settlements.

Jingu could not rule in her own right; her hope for an important future position lay in becoming pregnant. This might prove to be a difficult task. According to the *Nihongi* (720 A.D.) Chuai was in his early fifties at the time and already had two sons, either of whom could inherit his royal mantle. Having another heir by the new princess was not a pressing problem.

Chuai's Prime Minister and leading male shaman was "Valiant Old Bear Lord" or Takechiuchi no Sukune. He is postulated to have been sixth rank, one removed from the top five which could succeed to the kingship. From the events which unfolded, this prime minister-shaman seems to have been swept along with Jingu's ambitious plans for conquest and to have become her first lover.

Death and Prophecy

Japan's two earliest written records (712 and 720 A.D.) disagree about Chuai's death. (He did not die in bed of old age!) This king was purported to be attacking the Kumaso, a rebellious people living in south Kyushu. According to the *Kojiki*, when Chuai asked the "spirits" for a sign from the gods about his endeavors, the shaman-minister Takechiuchi "stood in the pure court" and asked for a sign from Heaven. This was Shamanist-type divination. Jingu "spoke with the mouth of the gods" and commanded Chuai to conquer "The Land of Across," which was filled with gold and silver. Chuai disbelieved this message, rebuking the gods for deceiving him. The king's refusal was followed by a dire prophecy spoken by Jingu as the mouthpiece of Heaven. It said that the disbelieving Chuai would not receive this new land, but the child in her womb, being a male child, would rule it.

Chuai, in his role as ruler of Koryong in central Korea, was not an absolute monarch, but more of a "first among equals" type of chieftain over a federation. The Kaya League was a widespread maritime conglomerate of small city-states. Either he felt lacking in

16

power or incentive.

The *Kojiki* states positively that Chuai died the same night that he refused to follow the commands of the gods, while playing a lute (*kayagum* in Korean, *koto* in Japanese). Chuai had received an unsettling prophecy that a child, who was destined for greatness, now grew within his beautiful, young wife. It would not be the first time a prophecy had scared a man to death.

It is more reasonable to speculate that Jingu, fed up with her marriage and secondary role, added something to the wine, with Takechiuchi being party to this, at least afterwards. According to the ancient historical records, both of them went to extreme measures to conceal Chuai's death until a later, more propitious time. (About a year later they ordered a tomb mound for him built in Kyushu, but the initial burial was secret. After the invasion was over, he was given the customary honors.)

Subjugation of Kaya (Silla)

After encompassing Chuai's death, young Jingu and "Valiant Old Bear Lord" seemingly knew they needed to hasten. They began to form an army of soldier-adventurers in the Tae Kaya area, with Koryong as its capital. Apparently messengers were sent to Paekche, with a deal for the monarch there: Support the endeavors of Jingu and she would conquer "The Land of Across" as Paekche's suzerain and also bring the Kaya League territory under its sway.

The *Nihongi* of 720 A.D. gives Jingu's route

opposite page, above left
Haniwa shaman with bells on his hat. This reflects the costumes worn by males when shamanizing in both old Korea and Japan during the proto-historic age.
opposite page, above right
Haniwa figure playing a kayagum. The invention of this instrument is credited to the Kaya kingdom.
opposite page, bottom
Koguryo musicians painted on a 4th-century tomb mural.

of conquest, beginning with Koryong (Taegu) and continuing southward, overrunning the Kaya League cities and pushing the resisting remnants up the eastern coast of Korea. The route followed is reasonable and militarily brilliant. However, in order to make Jingu a Japanese, the court histories needed to start Jingu from Kyushu and take her to Koryong and then backtrack southward. (In other words she passed peacefully over south Korean territory, and then reversed her route, fighting all the way.)

An interesting little indication of Jingu's ancestral roots in the extreme north, near the mighty Yalu River, someway crept into the *Nihongi* and has been preserved. (Perhaps not being understood?) It goes as follows: When Jingu subjugated "the King of Silla," he promised to faithfully serve her as a vassal "until the River Arinarae" runs backward in its course. Aston, the *Nihongi*'s translator, had no nationalistic ax to grind, and he considered this river to be the Yalu, which forms the western half of the present border of North Korea. Would Jingu, if she were indeed a native of Japan, have even heard of this river? Why should she consider an oath by this remote northern spot especially binding? The "King of Silla" might have knowledge of this river in memories which the Eastern Puyo had brought down to Kaya with them. The oath indicates that the king of the territory referred to as "Silla" in later times (eighth century) and Jingu shared a common heritage. This appears to have been their most sacred oath, for the "Dragon King of the Yalu River" was the most powerful of inland water deities. (Everyone, high or low, followed Shamanism as a religion in the mid-fourth century in this part of northeast Asia.)

It should be noted that since the Kaya territory was fought over by both Silla and Paekche during the fifth and sixth century,

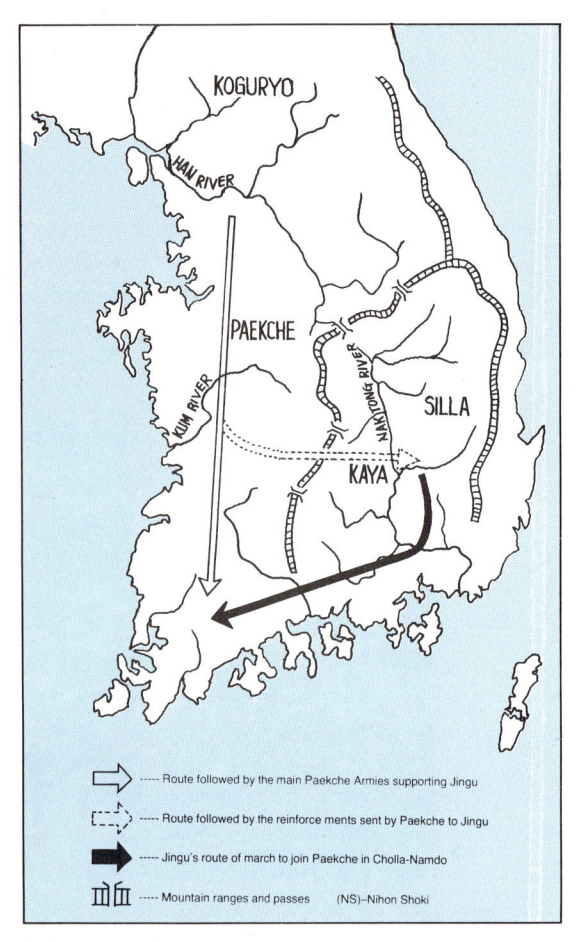

This map of Jingu's conquest, as recorded in the Nihongi, was first completed by a Korean scholar named Chon Kwan-U. The "route of conquest" given in the Nihongi is actually listed as a reconquest, but the origin of the conquerors is evident as being in the old Tae Kaya area (now Taegu).

and finally incorporated into Silla, the eighth-century historians' references to "Silla" may really concern Kaya territory in a geographic sense.

The Invasion of Japan

With "Valiant Old Bear Lord" as military advisor, augmented by troops and good wishes from Paekche, and also help from Silla, Jingu's plans for conquest of "The Land of Across" went smoothly. According to both

Paektu, or "Whitehead" mountain in North Korea. This extinct volcano with its crater lake is the source of the headwaters of both the Yalu and Tumen rivers. A great deal of magical symbolism and mystery surrounds this mountain.

court histories of the eighth century, "Silla sent eighty tribute ships" filled with silver and gold. This would seem to be literary hyperbole. Ships were certainly needed to carry out the first amphibious landing in numbers attempted in this part of the world. The naval armada had a special aura of invincibility; it was led by a shamaness-princess who believed she was ordered by the gods to conquer this land for her unborn son. Kaya League had many men with maritime know-how that Jingu could use.

Each ship, (based on measurements of the *Karano*, a contemporary ship) was quite large, and probably could hold approximately twenty horses and forty men, while carrying enough provisions to last the voyage, with a stopover for water in Tsushima. (The Chinese characters which make up the name of this island can read "Rival Horse.")

Even if fifty percent of the boats were lost due to storms, or unable to continue from Tsushima, this would still have left 800 horses and 1,600 men, quite a force when invading an island which was basically unfamiliar with cavalry tactics. It was the horse-oriented nature of this "invasion" that enabled Jingu's forces to unify much of the Japanese islands. Mere "boats" were for merchants and small bands of immigrant-settlers. The "Horseriders" were serious to conquer "new lands."

These early boats, as shown by some pottery models, had a front area which might be lowered like the ramp of a World War Two landing craft. The horse would then be mounted, jerked sideways, and charged off through the surf if necessary, the riders lopping off arms and heads on the way.

The foot-soldiers, having mounted their shields on the sides of the boats for protection, could lay down a murderous archery fire in a 180 degree arc on the defenders, being themselves hard to hit behind their iron shields.

The horses were armored like four-legged tanks, and just about as difficult for an unarmored foot soldier to stop. To get at the rider, the foot-soldier would need to swing his arms over his head, leaving his entire chest area open for attack. Both the court histories *(Kojiki* and *Nihongi)* report that Jingu and her fleet arrived in Kyushu without damage. She there gave birth to her boy child, later known as Ojin, who was, as the gods had prophesied, destined to rule this "Land of Across."

above
Haniwa boat (Tokyo National Museum), a 40-inch long model of a type probably used in the proto-historic period. Two rows of horses would be lined up nose to tail, crossways in the boat, to prevent them from falling overboard. Outboard walkways and a center aisle provided servicing areas. This boat was excavated from a Kyushu island tomb.
below
Haniwa horse. Jingu's forces' strength lay in cavalry tactics and horses. A parallel would be Cortez, who overcame the Aztec nation of Mexico with 200 men. Gumma Prefectural Museum.

The "Love Child" and His Conception

When the shamaness-princess announced that she was pregnant by King Chuai, she was making a claim to the throne, not just the Kaya League part but the "new lands to be conquered." It was more than nine months later that Jingu gave birth. The *Nihongi* indicates that her pregnancy lasted over ten months. This is explained by having her insert rocks in her loins to delay the birth beyond its normal time. (Myths handed down through the centuries show the Puyo worshipped rocks.)

However, for those who are more practically minded, another explanation exists. About a month after the death of Chuai, Jingu went into a Shamanistic seance to ask the gods which deity had commanded her to "conquer." The deity of the Cleyaera, the five-hundred branched *sakaki* tree, appeared as the Goddess of Mukatsu, "The Land of Across," commanding her to take control of this area. This Shamanist divination took seven days and seven nights; Jingu was accompanied by the shaman-minister "Valiant Old Bear Lord," and a Nakatomi, a ritualist.

Since this shaman-minister and Jingu were alone several times after Chuai's death, besides being its only witnesses, the likeliest biological father is this "Valiant Old Bear Lord." He was Jingu's chief support in her plan to conquer the new land. Even though Chuai had been removed from the scene, this minister could not rule in his own right, because his hereditary rank was too low. However, his child could secretly become a king,

top
Armored horse and rider, 4th or 5th century tomb, Koguryo.
middle
Flying shaman mural, Koguryo tomb.
bottom
Haniwa of a female shaman with tiger and leopard skin robe. Tokyo National Museum.

above
Kaya sword hilt in Kyongbuk University Museum, Taegu.
right
Sword hilt in Japan's Chiba Prefectural Museum. (Compare with Kaya sword hilt).

although officially Chuai's heir.

All accounts emphasize that Jingu was young, unbelievably beautiful, an accomplished shamaness. "Valiant Old Bear" had many women and founded six major clans with his children, but Jingu could offer him an unusual opportunity.

Apparently this Jingu was a strong woman, for even after she was supposed to be four months pregnant, she defeated a rival shaman who is described as "having wings on his body," coupled with the ability to fly. He refused Jingu's commands, so she killed him. The *Nihongi* lists her delivery of Ojin as the twelfth month, the fourteenth day. Chuai is recorded as dying the second month, the fifth day. This is explained in the *Nihongi* as follows: (under ninth month, eighth day):

> The time had now come for the Empress' delivery. So she took a stone which she inserted in her loins, and prayed, saying — 'Let my delivery be in this land on the day that I return after our enterprise is at an end.'

The "rock" is reported to have been egg-shaped. To rule Japan, Ojin needed to be born there, and not in Korea!

Battles and Deceit

Three months after landing in Kyushu, Jingu's forces confronted Chuai's two older sons who had also come to Japan, possibly by way of the Silla settlement at Izumo. Jingu's squadron of boats set "Valiant Old Bear Lord" or Takechiuchi ashore near modern Osaka, from which he moved inland to meet the two princes and their forces. The child Ojin had been given over to Takechiuchi's care.

At first the two princes had the upper hand, so Jingu's troops were told to tie extra bowstrings in their hair and gird on wooden swords when coming to the battleground, which was separated by a river. Then Takechiuchi called out to Chuai's two sons, "Why should I contend with thee? Let us cut our bowstrings, fling away our weapons and be in harmony with each other." Takechiuchi commanded his men to cut their bowstrings and fling away their swords in the river. The other side then did likewise. Then Takechiuchi commanded his men to bring out their spare bowstrings and "gird on their real swords." (The *Nihongi* does not explain where the swords had been hidden.) Need-

21

less to say Jingu's forces under Takechiuchi won the day. The two rivals were killed.

Jingu Received "Seven-Branched Sword" from Paekche

Among the most interesting presents mentioned in the ancient chronicles as sent by the Paekche court to Jingu was a strange object called "a seven-branched sword and a seven-little-one-mirror, with various other objects of great value." The intriguing fact is that two objects still exist in Japan, both designated as "National Treasures" which fit this description and are obviously dated in this early time. This "present" came in 372 A.D. according to the *Nihongi*. King Kunchogo of Paekche, who had apparently blessed her expedition, died three years later.

The only sword in all Japan with "seven branches" or seven pinnacles is the one now revered at Iso-no-Kami. The "seven branches" represent the "seven heavens" in Shamanist symbolism. Both the King of Paekche and Jingu of Japan were devout believers in Shamanism. This "seven" represents the "seven heavens" in which many tribes believed. The same "seven branches" can be seen on most of the golden crowns unearthed from Kyongju's fifth-century tombs. (Later both Korea and Japan were to become Buddhist and people forgot about this Shamanist symbolism and how strong it had once been.)

The major problem seems to be: Did Jingu actually bring this sword with her, as a present from the King of Paekche, wishing her well on her voyage? (The date on the sword reads 369 A.D.) Or is the *Nihongi* correct in saying that the sword arrived in 372 A.D.? Perhaps it is wrong? Or else, this sword was a sort of mark of approval sent to Jingu after she was successful?

According to Chon Kwan-u's translation, the inscription in Chinese reads:

Japan's only seven-branched or pronged sword, kept within the sacred precincts of Iso-no-Kami. This sword has several origins, depending upon which legend is followed, but the Nihongi assigns it as a present to Empress Jingu from Paekche. Length 74.5 cm. (The Puyo National Museum has a replica exhibited near its entrance.)

As this seven-branched sword has a magical power enabling its bearer to evade the blows of a sharp sword, we send it to the ruler of a vassal state. (literally, it would be good that a gift should be made of it to a vassal state). The Crown Prince of Paekche made it for the ruler of Wai.

Two reasons might account for the sword being made and presented to Jingu by the "crown prince" rather than the king of Paekche. The older king was quite busy fighting and had routed Koguryo soldiers who had come southward. King Kunchogo attacked Pyongyang and killed its then reigning king, Kogugwon. Paekche was at the height of its power in the late fourth century. Japan under Jingu was its "vassal state."

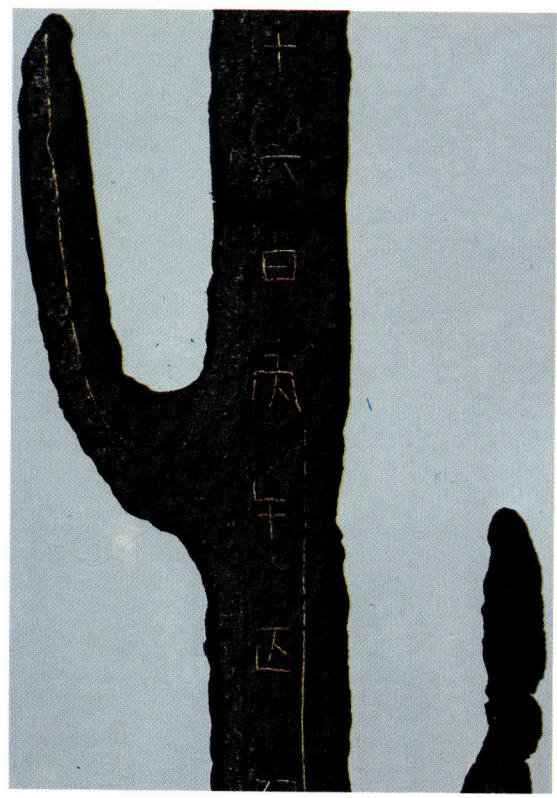

Closeup of Japan's seven-branched sword, with Chinese characters in the iron base, showing Paekche's metalworking technique in 369 A.D.

Bronze Mirror, Hachiman Shrine, Wakayama, National Treasure #131. Separate groups of stories seem to form the basis for Japan's Creation Myth.

Naturally Japanese scholars try to turn the inscription around and have Paekche the "vassal state" ruled by Jingu. She and Takechi-uchi were having trouble just holding together the central part of Japan!

"Seven Little One Mirror" from Paekche

A bronze mirror 20 cm. in diameter (less than a foot) is now designated as "National Treasure #131" and preserved at Hachiman Shrine, Wakayama. It has a number of scenes on its back side, which are connected with early mythology of the Sun Goddess and the Storm God. Can this be the mirror sent by Paekche's royal house to Jingu? (Her son later was idealized as Shintoism's Hachiman, God of War, which would explain the presence of the mirror at a Hachiman Shrine.) Or is this mirror an ancient copy of a "seven-little-one mirror?" The inscription upon it can be translated as "in the sheep year" which makes it 383, 443 or 503 A.D. The earliest possible date (383 A.D.) comes at the close of Jingu's reign, when Ojin was about to take over as ruler.

Inscription of 48 Characters

The Chinese lettering around the edge is somewhat ambiguous. It reads:

> In the year of the sheep, period of Great King, to a brother king in the south, when he was staying at Ishisaga Palace, thinking of longevity. He ordered two men to make

23

This closeup of the Hachiman Mirror, shows the Sun Goddess being lured from the "Heavenly Rock Cave" by a figure which has bared its breasts, along with a smaller figure holding the Yasaka Jewels.

this mirror, taking 200 *cho* of white nickel bronze.

Can this be the present from Paekche referred to in the *Nihongi*? Or a present of a large mirror from Paekche to Ojin, referred to in the *Kojiki*? Is the "king in the south" the ruler in Japan? (Kyushu is south of Paekche. Envoys found easiest sailing to go to Kyushu first from Paekche, and then use the Inland Sea to Osaka, anciently called Naniwa).

Mythological Scenes

The crimes of Susa-no-o the Storm God, are portrayed. He is shown riding his piebald colt through the Heavenly Ricefields of the Sun Goddess, his sister. Another scene shows Amaterasu being lured from her Rock Cave, her hiding place. Next is the bare-breasted, mischievous *kami* whose dance aroused laughter and brought the Sun Goddess out of her cave. The dancer holds a long string of the curved jewels or "Yasaka jewels" (*magatama*) which can be clearly seen hanging from her hands.

Another scene represents the Opening of the Heavenly Rock Bridge with a second bare-breasted female, the one who "shocked the guardian of the bridge" into dropping his trident spear. Next portrayed on the mirror is the Descent of Ninigi, the Imperial Grandson, to the Central Reed Plain. The Tearing of Susa-no-o's hair and his banishment are also given. Depending on how one divides up the spaces, either five or seven "scenes" can be counted around the inner circle.

These ancient legends, part of the mythological background of Japan's "unbroken line for ages eternal" are here on this mirror embossed on its unyielding bronze surface. Were the mirrors which became "sacred to the Sun Goddess" similar to this? Is this Hachiman mirror related to a large mirror which came out of Nintoku's Tomb when it was damaged in 1872 A.D.? (It is said that an ancient Japanese mirror now in the Boston Museum of Fine Arts came out at this time.) Just how much of Japan's ancient mythology came from Korea?

2 OJIN: FRIEND OF PAEKCHE

Jingu's Son, Ojin, Consolidates Power

Out of respect for the dynamic, charismatic shamaness-queen, who was ruling as regent for her son, "the emperor of the womb," the *Nihongi* has her die at one hundred. However, she seems to have been regent for twenty years, and then let Ojin assume power. Jingu's lover (Ojin's father?) is given even greater honor. He is recorded as advisor to about five emperors, living roughly three centuries. Apparently his descendants, taking the same name, did become sort of hereditary prime ministers for a while. The "Valiant Old Bear Lord" was a veritable stud, starting the family lines of a number of clans which became potent in Japan's government. The Puyo-Kaya line played a major role for several centuries. Thus Ojin was the first of a line of ten "emperors" with Horserider blood who occupied the throne of Japan from the late fourth century to 510 A.D. Then a compromise candidate was put on the throne. His descent was half-Horserider, the other half tracing back to Yayoi-period Korean immigrants to Japan (Shintoist powers).

At first Horserider emperors kept up connections with Kaya, and some of their wealth came from maritime connections there. Also their political ties were with Paekche, more than with Silla.

Ojin and Trial by Ordeal

The soldiers who had been left in Kyushu sometimes became restless. "Valiant Old Bear Lord" was accused of plotting with them, (The accuser was his own younger brother) so the ruler Ojin first ordered Takechiuchi killed. Later he was summoned for trial, but Takechiuchi was equal to this "trial by ordeal." During Europe's medieval period, trial by boiling water was also used. Two contestants would both plunge their

Haniwa ruler (Tenri Museum, Nara). This crown has uprights like the Kaya crown now in the Hoam Museum near Seoul.

arms in boiling water. The one whose cause was just (whom the gods favored) would be spared. Here Takechiuchi's Shamanist abilities gave him an advantage over his accuser, his younger brother. Mastery over fire is a common ability of shamans. (Apparently the secret of Ojin's birth was never disclosed to the ruler himself.)

Paekche's Gifts to Ojin

It seems apparent that Paekche recognized the new rulers in Japan as suzerain in a remote kind of way, and so sent goods and personnel to the islands in efforts to cement friendly relations. Chinese, Korean and Japanese histories consider all exchanges as

Haniwa horse (Tokyo National Museum) with saddle bows and bells found throughout Korea's Three Kingdoms' tombs.

The Chinese ideographs for "Heaven" and "Earth," the first two found in the basic Confucian primer, the 1000 Character Classic, brought to Japan in 405 A.D.

"tribute," implying a secondary relationship for the contributors, especially if directed towards China. But these "tributary missions" were really a form of international trade and did not necessarily reflect a vastly inferior position between countries.

During Ojin's reign a number of families came from Paekche and settled in Japan, and such skilled personnel as seamstresses were imported. The *Nihongi* mentions "The King of Paekche sent A-chik-ki with two quiet horses as tribute." Ojin discovered that this groom could read Chinese. The ruler questioned him about obtaining another learned man from Paekche who could read. A calendar was also needed to keep track of time. A number of ladies began to be exchanged between Japan and Paekche, as part of marriage politics, and this custom continued with each reign, as did the use of royal hostages in the person of younger brothers or cousins of the ruler. (This occurred on each side).

Chinese Letters Arrive from Paekche

Wani arrived in 405 A.D. to become the ancestor of Japan's Writers' Guild, or official scribes. This wedge of continental learning into the Japanese court may not have been the first time when Chinese writing came, but this date marks its lasting effect. The *Nihongi* states that Wani became the teacher of Japan's heir apparent, planting knowledge of older civilizations in his mind, as well as the Paekche way in which Chinese teachings had been adapted to suit the peninsula.

Ojin Popularized as Shinto's "God of War"

With the passage of time, Ojin, Japan's first Horserider emperor, became merged with the God of War in the Shinto pantheon, or Hachiman. Was this because the Horseriders were associated with conquest?

At important Hachiman shrines even today, the entrance is guarded by two large, fierce looking statues representing dogs, but sort of super-dogs. They are called *Koma-inu* or "Korean dogs." Confusion exists as to their meaning. Apparently in the northern part of Korea, dogs were interbred with wolves to make them fierce as guard dogs. Some may

above
Hachiman Shrine built by Minamoto Yoritomo in Kamakura. As God of War, Ojin the Horserider had many legends grow up about him, one of which has him riding a "red-soil horse" in the vicinity of his tomb upon occasion.

right
Koma Inu, from Kamakura's Hachiman Shrine. The term literally means "dog from Koguryo" as opposed to the totality of the Three Kingdoms. Apparently, the Horseriders brought wolf-dogs, who guarded early Shaman-Shinto shrines.

have been brought across in the boats with Jingu's forces. Eventually this special breed died out, but has been perpetuated in sculpture to guard Hachiman shrines. In later centuries military leaders of Japan often prayed at Hachiman shrines before setting out on an expedition. (Minamoto Yoritomo in particular valued Hachiman's help, according to histories of Japan's medieval period.)

Cultural Dependence upon Korea

Little if any direct contact occurred between Japan and China at this time because boats could just not set sail from Japan and expect to reach China. The *Nihongi* mentions the trouble involved in obtaining two seamstresses from China. Japan had to send two Koreans by boat to Koguryo, to ask help. That king there furnished two guides to conduct the Paekche men to China. The *Nihongi* does not say whether this was by coasting vessel or overland.

Craftsmen are mentioned over and over as having come from Korea, either as residents from there or passing through the peninsula on their way from China. The Horserider court was very dependent upon the Korean peninsula. At first, textile workers were much needed to ply and teach their special skills.

Women as Special Gifts

Marriage politics played a large part in royalty's lifestyle during this era, as it still does in Japan. For example, it is reported that the King of Paekche sent his younger sister as a consort for Ojin. Women were traded back and forth almost like livestock, but they were not just helpless slaves. The career of Jingu had started in much the same way.

When a princess royal was sent to "wait upon" the ruler of another land, she was accompanied by a large train of her serving women. They could serve in effect as an intelligence corps. Their bodily charms might ferret out information to relay to the princess; she could then advance her own position vis-a-vis the other consorts. If she gained the ruler's attention, she could shape events, or possibly produce an heir.

Shamanist Beliefs and Horserider Tombs

In the more than a century when the pure Horserider rulers were dominant in Japan,

Courtesans, wearing Korean costumes, from the recently excavated Takamatsu Tomb, Asuka. Even though this painting is 300 years after Ojin, Korean nobility in Japan still followed ancient traditions.

religious beliefs were 100 percent Shamanist. It was generally believed that when a human being died, he went to an afterlife not too different from earthly existence, accompanied by the goods which had been put in his grave for use in the hereafter. Naturally the higher the rank the larger the tumuli which could be constructed and the more grave goods would be interred along with the body. As

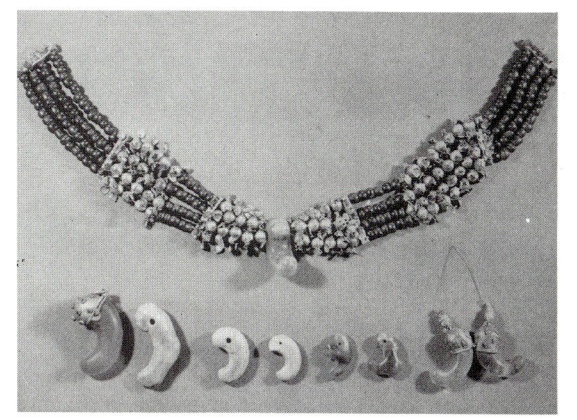

above left
Ladies-in-waiting wearing pleated skirts, from a 5th-century Koguryo tomb.
above right
The "comma-shaped jewels," (known as magatama in Japan and kokok in Korea) are common to both Japan and Korea, but not China. These are the "Yasaka Jewels" of the Sun Goddess.
below left
This Sue pottery stoneware vessel would be filled with a food or drink offering, to be used by the deceased in the afterlife. (Kaya stoneware fathered Sue pottery.) One of these vessels has as a decoration a boat, occupied by two men and two horses. Kyoto University Archeological Museum.
below right
Kaya stoneware vessel. Pusan University Archeological Museum.

"spirits" after death, the rulers would be expected to eat (so they needed food offerings), to drink (so wine must be provided), to play games, make love, hunt, fish, etc.

When still in the north, the Horseriders had been escorted in death with a large group of living wives, food, actual horses, and other status symbols. The interiors of the tombs would be painted (in both Altai and Korean traditions) with scenes from the deceased ruler's life on earth, plus projected scenes of the afterlife along with the four sacred animals of the four directions. The ruler was buried with symbols of power such as his personal sword, bows and arrows, even his ceremonial shoes. Jewelry, fabricated from gold and silver, adorned the corpse in Korea where such metals were plentiful. (Apparently Japan was short of these materials, so gilt bronze was substituted.)

The food offerings were cooked and placed in stoneware vessels raised on pedestals. Potters from Kaya had accompanied the Horseriders, for their skills were needed to please the gods, both before a battle and for grave goods. Since drinking was among the Horserider's favorite indoor occupations, wine vessels of stoneware were included in the tomb apparel.

At some time, the former practice of burying actual horses and people was given up and clay statuettes substituted. The "double mound" or keyhole shape was supposed to be reserved for rulers, but some of the clan nobles in Kyushu also built large tombs and used the double mound. (A number of double mound or key-hole shape tombs stretch from Kongju down to Pusan, but many of them have been encroached upon by rice fields.)

Tomb of Ojin (See Map)

As the first official ruler of a new line of kings, Ojin's tomb needed to be splendid for

An armored haniwa (Arikawa Archeological Museum) which became a substitute for the human sacrifices carried out by the early Horseriders. This same type of costume can be seen in the Grand Procession on page 12.

the sake of prestige and to stamp his dynasty with permanence. His reign was fairly peaceful; the older clan leaders, resident in Japan, had themselves remote Korean ancestry, having fought their way to dominance by overcoming the Stone Age earlier inhabitants. Local clan chieftains were regranted their fiefs in exchange for cooperation.

The mound assigned by tradition to Ojin measures 419 meters long and has a height of 35.8 meters (over a hundred feet). Including the moat, this tomb stretches 500 meters in overall length. Perhaps it once had three moats. During the middle ages all the imperial tombs were neglected, but after the revi-

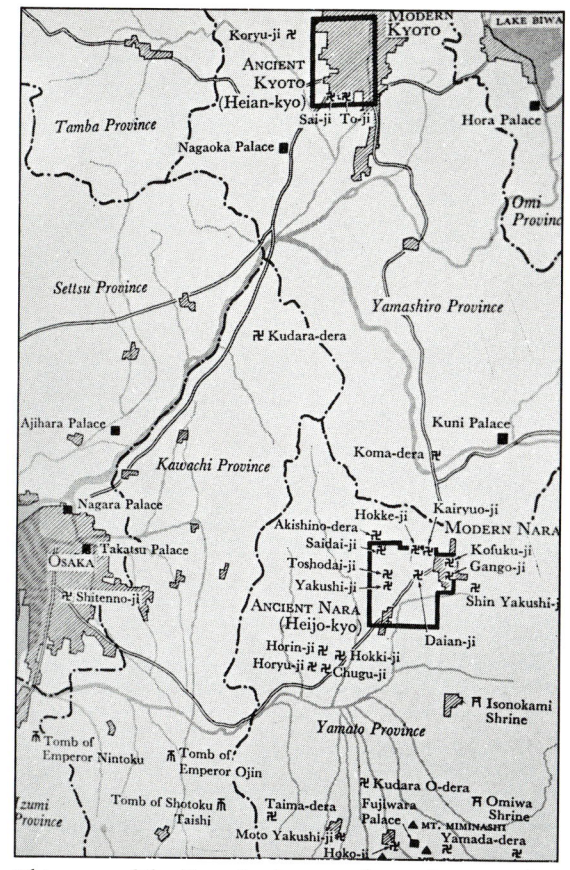

This map of the Nara-Asuka area shows the spread of huge tombs in Japan's proto-historic, or Horserider Age.

Aerial photo of the tomb assigned to Sujun, Emperor #29. The tomb of Ojin was much larger, but similar in construction. All suggest continental antecedents.

val of Shintoism under Emperor Meiji, the tombs were leveled and cleared, Today occasional offerings are made on a stone altar erected on the square end. Ojin's tomb has now been made a sanctuary stretching about 700 meters from north to south (about five city blocks) and is 620 meters from east to west.

One can assume that such tombs required the labor of many men on corvée duty, or perhaps slaves taken as prisoners of war. Moats were excavated as protection from evil spirits as well as grave robbers. Soil taken from the moats could be used to erect the tumuli. The moats could be filled from the small streams that crisscrossed this area near Osaka.

In modern times Shinto court officials make annual pilgrimages to this and other tombs in the Asuka area, offering products of the mountains, the rivers and seas, to represent land and water. The death anniversaries are followed as given in the *Nihongi,* the court history completed in 720 A.D.

Few, if any, court officials even realize the possibility that such tombs belong to a line of "foreign conquerors." Although the branches were sometimes remote, still, in a sense, Ojin's line continued on the throne for a very long time.

3 NINTOKU: DIVINE DESPOT

Nintoku and Contest for the Throne

Throughout Asia the various horseriding nomads rarely had strict rules of primogeniture. Therefore, on the death of a ruler, a contest often developed. One or two charismatic leaders would put a large group of followers together and acquire territory, only to have its strength lessened by quarrels over the succession, with much bloodletting. Japan's new nomadic line proved no exception; almost every reign saw trouble.

The *Nihongi* states that Ojin asked his sons, which should rule, the older or younger. Nintoku, the oldest, realized that his father favored the younger son. According to the account both deferred to the other, but this is just a coverup. Nintoku established his capital at Naniwa (or Osaka) and the younger brother at Uji. Finally the younger brother "took his own life," so as to force Nintoku to rule. This is obviously a nice way of putting it. The writers go on to flatter Nintoku, and say that he didn't collect taxes for three years, or have his "palace" repaired even though its roof leaked. However, almost identical passages occur in Chinese history books, and this seems to have been merely copying.

Palace Architecture

Actually the ruler's "palace" was not too different in architectural style from a Shinto shrine. Both were larger than the peasant's hut, but not fancy or vast from a modern point of view.

Rectangular buildings were constructed of wood, somewhat like a log cabin, supported by pillars planted directly in the ground. (The custom of using stone foundations for the pillars did not begin until the late sixth century when Paekche temple architecture was followed.)

Cords of long-stemmed climbing vines held together the post, rafters, beams and even door frames. These buildings were so flimsy that they could not last much more than two decades. (Ise Shrine is rebuilt every twenty years even today, perhaps reflecting this early era.) The palace building was thought to be contaminated after the death and funeral of a ruler. The new incumbent on the throne then built or ordered built another "palace" in a slightly different place.

The Horseriders had lived in the saddle at one time, so elaborate buildings for this life were not important, but they did believe in more permanent homes for the afterlife. During the period of over a century, when the descendants of Jingu and Ojin were ruling central and western Japan, the valley of Asuka,

opposite page
Armored haniwa, drawing his sword, excavated in Gumma Prefecture. Tokyo National Museum.
above
Haniwa (Arikawa Archeological Museum) wearing a crown similar to the Kaya crown in the Hoam Museum, Yongin, Kyonggi-do.

above
Haniwa building showing Iron Age architecture.
below
In the inner circle of the mirror, different buildings can be seen. It is quite certain, by looking at Ise Shrine, that this mirror suggests the Horseriders' "palace architecture." Tokyo National Museum.

stretching towards Osaka, came to be filled with dozens of tombs for the Horserider rulers, their consorts and their high officials. Many still survive. However, the government prevents archeological excavations upon these, although permitting the tombs in Kyushu of the nobles there to be explored.

Marriage to the "Rock Princess"

Nintoku seems to have been concerned with commerce, and thus moved his capital to the port of Naniwa on the Inland Sea. He also married Iwa no Hime, or "Princess of the Rock," from southern Korea. Throughout the *Nihongi*, the mention of rocks is often connected with miracles. The original "Descent from Heaven" of the Sun Goddess' offspring was made in "Heavenly-Rock Boats." A boat could hardly be carved from rock, but the magic power of "rock" is evident.

The Rock Princess was famed for her jealousy. This woman restrained her hus-

33

left
This haniwa falconer fits exactly a description in the Nihongi for Prince Chu's bird, Yamato Bunka-kan, Nara.
above
Falconer painted in a 5th-century Koguryo tomb mural.

band's roving eyes as much as possible, even to the point of leaving him forever when Nintoku took another consort. She sailed away from his palace and remained away for thirty-three years, the rest of her life!

Falconing Comes from Paekche to Osaka

It is written in the *Nihongi* that a Paekche prince was disrespectful to Japan and delivered over to Japanese envoys in chains. He soon ran away and remained in hiding until forgiven. This may be a literary coverup for a prince who was shipped away from Paekche for fomenting rebellion, or disliking the idea of royal hostages. But he seems to have been a prince, for he introduced falconry to Japan.

A huntsman captured a strange bird in a net, and presented it to the emperor for his pleasure. Lord Chu, the Paekche prince, was summoned since obviously he would have wider knowledge of such things than a native. The bird seems to have been a peregrine falcon, which Lord Chu promptly trained for

above
A keyhole-shaped tomb near Kongju, second capital of the Paekche Kingdom, indicates the technology to build these tombs derived from Korea, in spite of the "uniqueness" claim of Japanese scholars. More than a dozen of these tombs exist in the Paekche-Kaya area.
right
Aerial view of Emperor Nintoku's tomb, the largest in Japan.

hunting. He returned it to Nintoku with a leather strap to keep the falcon tethered to the wrist, and a small bell attached to its tail. After this, hunting falcons were imported to Japan from Paekche.

Nintoku went hunting upon the moor with his new pet and "caught several tens of pheasants," which delighted him. A falcon-keepers guild was established, no doubt with Prince Chu as its head.

Nintoku's "Great Tomb"

If the size of funeral mounds assigned to the Horseriders has any meaning, then Nintoku was the strongest of these rulers from the continent. The practice had begun centuries before in the Caucasus Mountains of erecting stone tomb chambers and filling the mound's top with rubble and small stones. This custom had traveled across Siberia. Today mounds can be seen all over the Korean peninsula, but none is as high or as extensive as the tumulus which Nintoku is said to have personally supervised for his own demise. (see front endpapers)

Nintoku's tomb is a little inland from Osaka, his capital. It stretches 475 meters long and originally was surrounded by three moats. Only one remains today, since later-day rice farmers gradually encroached on the other two moats, when respect for any emperor was not very high. It has been estimated that Nintoku's mound had 26,000 cubic meters of stone used for its inner structure, with then earth and later trees allowed to grow on top. Its area in its original state was half that of an Egyptian pyramid.

Nintoku's tomb is reported to have been encircled several times with *haniwa* (circles of clay) or cylinders created specially to go around the edge of tombs, to serve as

35

guardians. These earthenware *haniwa* often fell in the water of a moat and returned to clay. Some were taken away and saved during the centuries when shoguns rather than emperors ruled. Although the *Nihongi* states that 10,000 *haniwa* were used for Nintoku's tomb, none stand there today.

However, from his grave or those of others, many have been assembled in museums today, and reveal a great deal about the lifestyle and religious attitudes of the Horserider emperors and their subjects. (See illustrations)

Archeology Officially Discouraged

The Imperial Household still denies requests to investigate the tombs assigned to Ojin or Nintoku, saying "the sacred bones of the Emperor should not be disturbed." Even though the Imperial Presence is no longer held sacred, still an Iron Age aura of mythology hangs over the tombs. The archeologists from various universities, particularly in the Kyushu area, have been allowed to excavate tombs classified as having belonged to the nobility because they are less grandiose. The names assigned to the tomb mounds in the Nara-Osaka area are based on oral tradition, names which someway survived numerous centuries, when the imperial power was weak, and the shoguns were the most feared and respected rulers in Japan. However, just as the Nile in Egypt has its Valley of Kings, the largest mounds on the Japanese archipelago appear to be clustered around the Nara-Osaka-Asuka region.

According to Professor Ryusaku Tsunoda, a former Japanese history professor of Columbia University, when a storm damaged Nintoku's tomb in 1872:

> There was an opportunity, while repairs were being made, to look inside. People were amazed to see how many objects of continental craftsmanship it contained. The ruler... lived in the fourth century. The buried treasures were evidences of his relationship with the kingdoms of the Korean peninsula.

After viewing the fifth-century tombs of Kyongju, one can imagine that Nintoku's contained many similar objects, more primitive perhaps, since he lived a century earlier. The Horseriders probably did not have at their command as many skilled craftsmen as did the Silla kings at a later date.

One thing which should exist in all the major Horserider tombs would be a painting of the Flying White Horse of the Puyo. This horse with "eight legs" is a theme which stretches from the Altai region down to Kyongju. The stylistic renditions may be different, but the horse with the long, out thrust tongue and an upswept tail signified the speed of the shaman-ruler on his "heavenly missions." This flying horse would lead the royal van on its path to the final resting place in the afterlife.

Shinto shrines throughout Japan often have one small additional building which recalls the cult of the white horse. This is a box-stall type of shrine, inside which reposes a lifesize plaster or cement statue of a white horse, with a black mane and tail. The spot is encircled with Shinto's "sacred rope," which outlines the holy area. A wooden offering box has not been forgotten; it stands in front of the horse's head — what prayers are now said to it are unknown.

Scholarly Pursuits Begin Displacing Martial Arts

The early formerly nomadic kings were illiterate; Wani, coming from Korea (405 A.D.) began the writer's guild. Over a period of time, conditions changed with the arrival of a constant stream of immigrants from the peninsula; they were awarded rank and noble status for their contributions of knowl-

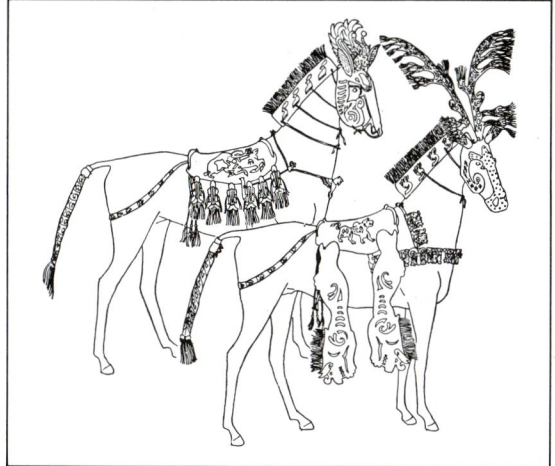

above
In the Takehara Tomb, Kyushu, stands a figure in continental Horserider dress, leading a horse ashore from a boat. Overhead soars Shamanism's Flying Horse. This is a crude representation of the Horserider's arrival.
below (bottom)
These flying horses from a Koguryo mural show the same characteristics as the ones in Silla and Japan.

above
This Kyushu tomb shows a basically identical design to Koguryo's corbelled tomb.
below
These Altai horses would lead the procession of the ruler to the afterlife. This grand procession is reminiscent in both form and substance of the tradition which demanded the building of the huge 5th-century tombs in Korea and Japan.

37

edge. For example, the Hata clan, which brought knowledge of weaving to the Horserider court, was entrusted with official records of expenditures, a sort of "county clerk." Another Korean family, the Soga, was given general supervision over all the storehouses. Gradually, a number of the elite immigrants from the continent learned to read and write Chinese; many of the nobility had Korean names. Even as late as 815 A.D., 30 percent of the nobility in Japan claimed non-Japanese ancestry in a census.

It is recorded in 495 A.D., the first of an annual "Winding Water Party" (*Gokusui-no-en*) took place. It was held on the third day of the third lunar month, an auspicious time. The invited lords and ladies were seated on straw mats alongside the banks of a flowing rivulet. Rice wine cups were floated down the stream, to be picked up, whereupon the recipient must compose a poem. It is notable that the Silla court also did this, and a winding-watercourse (*Posokjong*) is preserved to this day in Kyongju. The polish of civilization was smoothing the rough edges off the once-fierce Horseriders.

The Posokjong, a stone trough in which cups of wine floating about were connected with poetry competitions, shows that both Japan and Korea shared this type of royal activity. (Seoul's American Ambassador's residence has a modern replica.)

4 PUYO'S ROCK DEITY

Later Horserider Rulers

At the death of Horserider Emperor #2 (Nintoku), two of his sons struggled for the right to succeed. The winner was posthumously entitled Richu, and has been given the number 17 spot in Japan's official lineup of emperors. He reigned in the early fifth century A.D.

The Horseriders were slowly losing their nomadic ways, but not their love of liquor. According to the *Nihongi*:

> The heir was drunk and would not get up. Therefore, three men assisted the heir, making him mount on horseback and caused him to escape.

Richu's younger brother, in trying to assassinate his older brother, set fire to the palace. After escaping his would-be killers (and sobering up), Richu took refuge in the Shrine of Iso-no-Kami, as stated in the *Nihongi*. Iso-no-Kami, the Puyo's ancestral Rock Shrine was sacred, and therefore safe from attack. It was also an armory, where Richu and his partisans could gather weapons.

Richu and another younger brother conspired to have the would-be usurper eliminated by hiring an assassin. According to the *Nihongi*:

> Watching the time when the (rebellious younger brother) prince went into the privy he was stabbed to death.

It was now safe for Richu to leave Iso-no-Kami's sacred precincts and assume the "Imperial Dignity." Richu was a son of the Rock Princess; he made two descendants of Takechiuchi (leaders of the Heguri and Soga clan), his noble-administrators. Everything was in Horserider control.

After this narrow escape, Emperor Richu, feeling gratitude to the spirit of the Puyo's Rock Shrine, established his palace nearby.

left
Entrance to Iso-no-Kami Shrine, Nara Prefecture, as seen today.
above
This sword found in a Silla tomb is unique, suggesting the Horseriders' Scythian background. Such a sword would be an heirloom, passed down as a symbol of power to each ruler or "inheritor of the sword."

The palace of Richu was located at a place called "Ihare," which means "children of the Rock," or "Rock Family," or "Rocklings," signifying the Puyo. The legendary first emperor of Japan, known as "Jimmu Tenno," (his posthumous name) was also named "Ihare," and he appears to be a composite of several of the early Horserider emperors.

Three years after ascending the throne, Richu had a fresh water conduit excavated to Iso-no-Kami for the convenience of the shrine's keepers. Later, while sitting in his palace Richu heard:

A miraculous blast of wind which cried aloud in the great void saying. "Oh thou prince, inheritor of the sword!"

This formal title, was used by the deity to announce to Richu the death of an imperial concubine, a Chinese-Korean named Hata. At this time the belief in spirits was paramount; divination and oracles were used to judge future or past actions. On the peninsula,

The age-old cedar trees surrounding Iso-no-Kami Shrine, near present-day Tenri.

Koguryo and Paekche had accepted Buddhism, but in both Silla and the new kingdom of Yamato, shaman-kings still held power.

Japan's Capital Moved to Shrine of the Puyo Rock Deity

The sixth Horserider ruler was named Anko, or "Peace." But, in the fifth century there was anything but peace. Anko moved his capital to the sacred area surrounding the precincts of the Puyo's Rock Shrine.

The Horserider ruler's life was tempestuous. Anko had killed his older brother and taken his wife. When he went to "enjoy the hot baths" and was thus without his armor, the ruler was supposedly murdered by his seven-year old stepson, revenging the father's murder.

Rocks as a Sign of Puyo Legitimacy

Yuryaku, the eighth Horserider emperor is blackened in the *Nihongi* as bloody-handed, called "the greatly wicked emperor" by the people of the time. When Yuryaku came to power he slew all rival claimants to the throne, except for two nephews who escaped to Iso-no-Kami Shrine. On growing up, the two royal princes worked as farm boys near the shrine.

Later, an imperial messenger asked the boys to dance, and one, thinking he could bear exile no longer, composed this poem (as recorded in the *Nihongi*):

> The sacred cedar of Furu in Iso-no Kami
> Its stem is severed
> Its branches are stripped off,
> Of him who in the palace of Ichinobe
> Governed all under Heaven,
> The myriad heavens, the myriad lands,

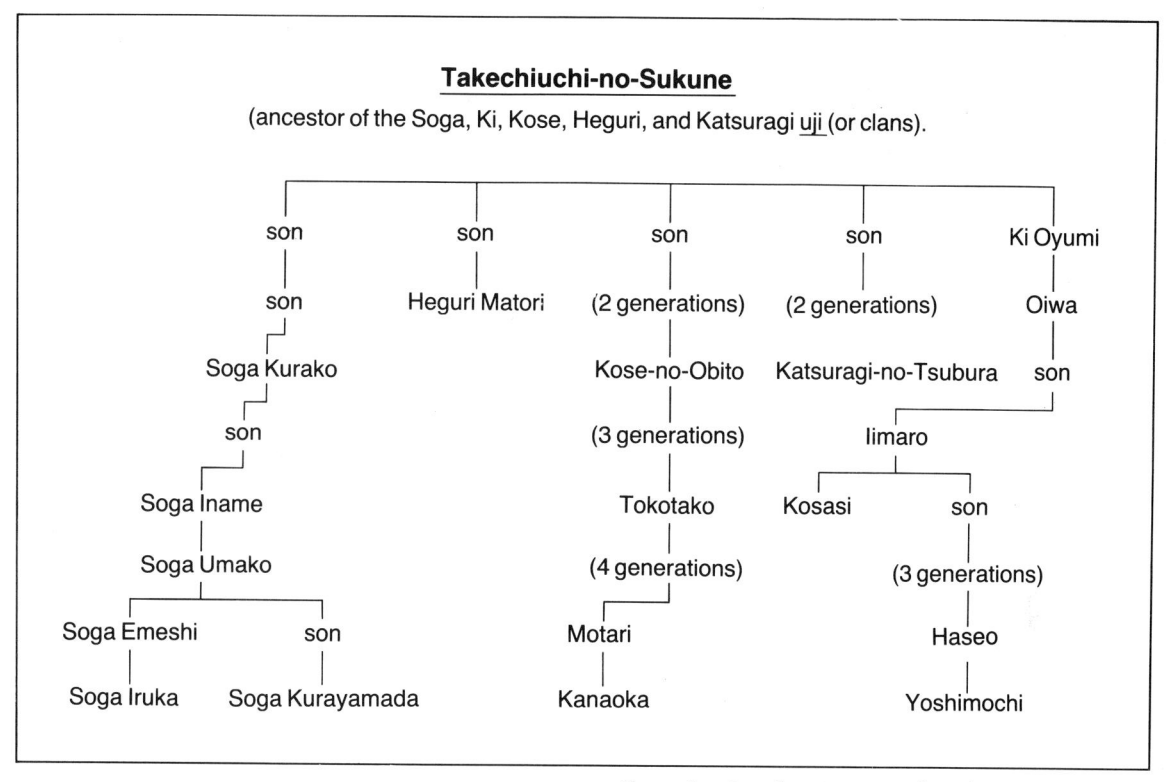

Takechiuchi-no-Sukune

(ancestor of the Soga, Ki, Kose, Heguri, and Katsuragi uji (or clans).

```
        ┌──────────┬──────────┬──────────┬──────────┐
       son        son        son        son       Ki Oyumi
        │          │          │          │          │
       son    Heguri Matori (2 generations) (2 generations) Oiwa
        │                     │          │          │
   Soga Kurako          Kose-no-Obito  Katsuragi-no-Tsubura  son
        │                     │          │
       son              (3 generations)  Iimaro
        │                     │        ┌──┴──┐
   Soga Iname             Tokotako   Kosasi  son
        │                     │                │
   Soga Umako           (4 generations)  (3 generations)
     ┌──┴──┐                  │                │
 Soga Emeshi  son          Motari           Haseo
     │        │               │                │
 Soga Iruka  Soga Kurayamada  Kanaoka       Yoshimochi
```

Chart showing the six major clans begun by "Valiant Old Bear."

Of Oshiha no Mikoto, the August Children are we.

This poem means that the two cowherds (later to reign as Kenso and Ninken) are the last two descendants of the Cosmic Tree of the Puyo line.

An interesting story which is recorded under Yuryaku's reign is that a man named Kunimi accused the keeper of the imperial bathhouse of having an affair with an imperial princess. The father of the attendant, in order to make amends, killed his son. Later, the father discovered that the princess had hung herself in shame. When the father cut open the abdomen of the suicide, he discovered a rock in the waters of her womb. The stone proved that both his son and the princess were innocent, for a stone symbolized an imperial child, from which the Puyo's "rock-lings" were born.

Puyo Rock Deity Shrine Decreases in Importance

Eventually the second of the two orphan emperors came to the throne as Ninken, in about 498 A.D. Perhaps in gratitude for the preservation of his life as a youth, Ninken made the Puyo's Rock Deity Shrine his capital. There had been an Iso-no-Kami Guild, and a prince given that name, but the Horserider rulers could no longer control the other noble clans. The totally Puyo-Horserider line founded by Jingu and Takechiuchi had by now begun to lose its strength.

As a final irony, during a later period, stewardship of the Iso-no-Kami Shrine was given into the care of the Mononobe clan, Horserider rivals, who later helped exterminate the last of the direct Horserider descendants, the Sogas.

Muretsu the Mad: A Literary Device?

Both the *Kojiki* and the *Nihongi* mention an emperor (#26) who appears to have been certifiably mad. Was this a literary device, such as used by Chinese histories to justify a change of dynasty? The *Kojiki* hardly does more than mention this ruler, but the *Nihongi* vilifies Muretsu with such explicit language, that Aston, translator of the *Nihongi,* rendered the obscene parts in Latin. This is the manner in which Chinese histories change dynastic records; the *Nihongi* then breaks from Book One to Book Two.

Muretsu is credited with assorted deeds that are reminiscent of Marquis de Sade. Men were shot down from trees with arrows. Muretsu had women ripped open to examine the state of the fetus in the womb. Also he forced women to copulate with horses.

Such defamation seems a device indicating dynastic change and the next emperor, Keitai, definitely was a compromise candidate. He carried both Wa-Japanese and Puyo-Horserider blood in his veins. Actually, the first candidate approached ran away and hid himself; being emperor was hazardous to one's longevity at times.

Keitai, the compromise candidate, also established his capital at Ihare ("Rockling"), where Jingu, Richu and Seinei had resided. This indicates that the new line of rulers had only partly shaken off the Horserider inheritance. Emperor #30, Bidatsu, raised his palace at Kudara (Paekche), but his successor went back to Ihare.

Distant view of Mt. Unebi and the Asuka Valley.

The new center of activities was to eventually become Asuka, about two and a half miles from the slopes of Mt. Unebi, where the tomb of the first Horserider from Korea is said to lie. The introduction of Buddhism in 552 A.D. was to lead to the pre-eminence of another group of Horserider descendants, members of the Soga clan, which stemmed from "Valiant Old Bear." Soga, patrons of art and religious politics, were to indelibly mark Japanese tradition during the sixth and seventh centuries, the "Soga dynasty" coming to an end in 646 A.D.

Part II Titlepage: Illustration of an 11th century screen entitled "Scenes from the life of Prince Shotoku." Here the regent is shown surrounded by his Korean monk-teachers at the first Horyu-ji, Wakakusa-dera.

PART 2

KOREANS AND JAPAN'S HISTORIC PERIOD

1 ASUKA AND EARLY BUDDHISM

Asuka: An Early Settlement for Korean Immigrants

The Yamato area became the powerbase for the Horseriders from the fourth century on; both the direct descendants of the emperors and the collateral and cadet branches clustered there. Most of the tombs of the longest-reigning rulers stand within the Asuka-Nara locale as does the sacred precincts of Iso-no-Kami Shrine, principal place of worship for the Puyo's Rock Deity. The earliest imperial palaces were located either near Asuka, or not far removed. Naniwa, later to become Osaka, served as the principal entry point for material goods imported from the continent, which would then come overland and by river barge to the civilization-hungry rulers and grandees of the Yamato court.

Keitai Tenno (reigned 507–531 A.D., listed as #26 in the official line) was placed on the throne as a compromise candidate, one with both Horserider blood and that of the earlier line. As empress, Keitai took the daughter of Ninken, last of Iso-no-Kami's "orphan emperors," no doubt thus sealing the bargain that placed him on the throne. The child of this union was later to rule in his own right as the Emperor Kimmei (#29), demonstrating the continuance of the Horseriders' lineage.

Soga's "Marriage Politics"

At the time of Kimmei (540–571 A.D.), Soga Iname got his "foot in the door" of the new imperial lineage, by providing a daughter to serve as consort of the reigning emperor. This daughter gave birth to seven sons and six daughters, two of them later rising to the throne of Japan. The Soga clan, one of the six started by "Valiant Old Bear" of the Horseriders, had been in and out of power since the time of Jingu, with the most senior

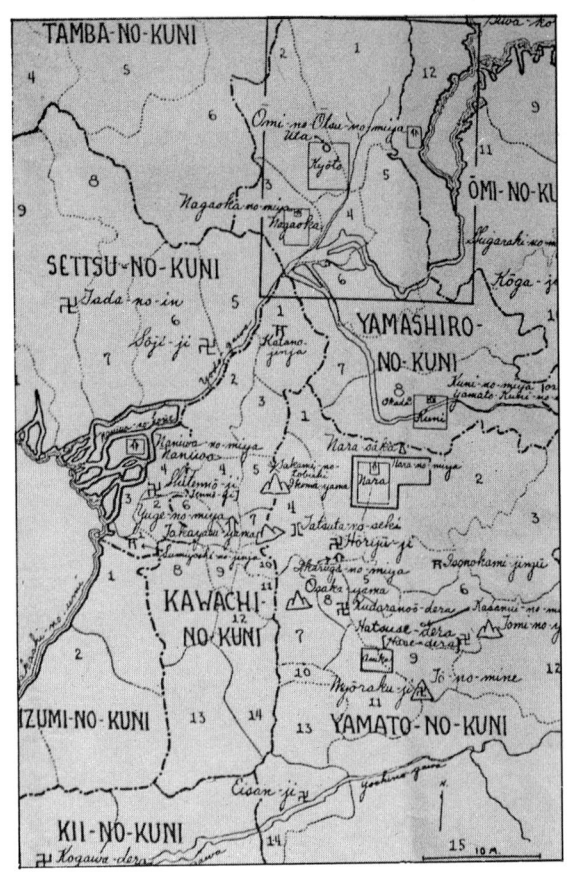

Drawing showing the location of various places mentioned in the text.

Soga male usually being the *Oho-Omi*, or head of civil as opposed to sacred affairs. Descendants of the Soga were to maintain a tight grip on the real power in Japan for more than a century. Marriage politics served the Soga power-brokers well; then the coming of Buddhism from Korea furthered the Soga cause.

Paekche's Introduction of Buddhism

During the reign of the Emperor Kimmei (540–571 A.D.), King Syong-myong of Paekche sent to the Japanese court, according to the *Nihongi* under the date 552 A.D.:

A present to the Emperor of an image of Shaka Butsu in gold and copper, several flags and umbrellas, and a number of volumes of "Sutras."

The King of Paekche is also recorded to have sent a laudatory memorial concerning the teachings of Buddhism, its superior nature philosophically, its uses in protecting the state and commonweal. One particular phrase which surely caught the attention of Emperor Kimmei was "Every prayer is fulfilled and naught is wanting." For a ruler descended from Shamanist nomads, the enticement of this sentence is obvious, for the deities of nature which these Shamanists worshipped were capricious and sometimes cruel. An appeal existed in receiving a new religion which was so powerful that it had spread from far-away India through China to Korea, where all of the Three Kingdoms now gave it reverence.

Buddhism Foments Internal Jealousies

The statement of the historical Buddha, "My Law Shall spread to the East," no doubt worried the pro-Shinto ritualists, especially the Nakatomi clan, whose historical role had been a Shamanistic interpretation of the "Divine Will of the Gods *(Kami)."* The Nakatomi saw in Buddhism the eventual destruction of their power-base in court and over the ruler. The Mononobe clan leader (head of the troops) also opposed Buddhism for much the same reason. Emperor Kimmei tried to be neutral; he allowed the Soga to worship the image only privately. (Soga Iname was his father-in-law.)

More than just the conflict of two types of religion is evident here; behind lay a power struggle between recent immigrants (Horse-rider descendants who were hungry for new cultural ideas from the continent) vs. Yeyoi-Korean strains (earlier immigrants who preferred to keep out new ideas which would disturb their ancient privileges).

This first entrance of Buddhist thought into the Japanese islands failed, for a plague

Fragment of a Buddhist banner, now in Tokyo National Museum. The original is a twenty-foot long sheet of metal, sent to Japan, housed for centuries at Horyu-ji.

which had already ravaged Japan increased in severity. The Shinto supporters in the persons of the Mononobe and Nakatomi, immediately blamed the heightened epidemic on the new foreign religion, which they believed to be displeasing to the native gods. The frightened emperor, swayed against Buddhism, let the Buddha image be thrown in the Naniha Canal, and the temple be burned which Soga Iname had erected as part of his own mansion. (These politically expedient acts did not benefit the conspirators much, for the plague then increased in severity, and inexplicably the Great Hall of Kimmei's palace burned down, "there being in the Heavens neither clouds nor wind.")

After these manifest signs of Heaven's displeasures, Kimmei then commissioned the carving of two Buddhist statues from a log of "magically shining" camphor wood that was found floating in the sea (drifting up from the south?). Camphor was to become a preferred material for Buddhist sculpture.

Paekche's Continuing Cultural Input

Over the centuries, Paekche had been the chief "cultural connection" between the isolated archipelago and the continent's progressive civilization. At the time of Buddhism's first abortive entrance, an envoy from Paekche returned to his homeland with a request from Kimmei for all kinds of Paekche men, those skilled in divination, calendar-making, medicine and literature. This added influx of traffic from the peninsula increased the activities around the Osaka port. Soga Iname maneuvered events so that he was placed in charge of shipping taxes; then he appointed a recent Korean immigrant to be in charge of the port itself. In this way the Sogas increased their revenues and also their contacts with the peninsula, from which their ancestors had come in 369 A.D.

Buddhism Used to Woo Japan's Court

Paekche wanted Japan as a military ally, so she continued to promote Buddhist knowledge at the court. When a new ruler came to the throne, Bidatsu (572–584 A.D.), Paekche sent over two hundred holy books (sutra), along with a meditative monk, a nun and a reciter of mantras (sutras based on the ability of sound to give magical power), plus a maker of Buddhist images and a temple architect. This was a nucleus for the construction of a temple and personnel to run it.

A Maitreya carved from granite, sent to Japan in 584 A.D. (according to the Nihongi) is missing, but the Kyongju National Museum exhibits a similar pose, albeit damaged. Soga Umako asked for the imported statue.

Silla, not to be outdone, sent to Japan a Buddhist image of its own. In 584 A.D., a bronze Buddha image and a stone icon of the Buddha-to-Come, Maitreya, are recorded as coming to Japan through a private citizen of Paekche. Probably other Buddhist paraphernalia arrived, which the court histories omit.

It should be noted that at this time a young princess of nineteen, daughter of Kimmei (ruler #29), had become a consort of Bidatsu (#30). She was Soga Iname's grandchild and was to rule later as Empress Suiko. It is her

This rock-cut Maitreya, still in situ in Chungchong Province, suggests what Soga Umako's "present" may have looked like.

Buddhism's powers, but they used it as a tool or a façade for their clan designs as well. The blood of "Valiant Old Bear" ran in their veins.

Soga Umako Speeds the Importation of Buddhist Influence

Soga Umako (whose Horserider lineage is apparent in his name, *Umako* means literally "Horse-Child") took the reigns of power from his father Iname as Chief Minister. Umako went to great lengths to promote Buddhism in Japan by requesting images and teachers from Koguryo, Paekche and Silla, even though his personal preference leaned towards Paekche.

In 584 A.D., two envoys from Paekche brought to Soga Umako a stone Maitreya the Buddha-of-the-Future who would come as Messiah, and a figure of Shakyamuni, the historical Buddha. Apparently, imports from Paekche alone were not enough to temper Umako's thirst for Buddhism, for he sent messengers out into the Japanese countryside to search out those who knew Buddhist teachings.

Minister Soga's messengers could only find one man from Koguryo, Hephyon, a monk who had returned to lay life. Soga Umako made of this lay priest a teacher, and sent a young girl to him to learn the ways of a nun. Two more pupils from noble families joined the nunnery that Soga Umako was now constructing on the east side of his house. (The disastrous fate of his father's first home-temple was firmly in mind!).

At this time, when Shinto-Shamanism still reigned in Japan, all natural objects were considered the dwellings of *kami* (spirits), and sacred swords and mirrors were in existence. Buddhism had its own fashion of holy relics and magic. Shiba Tatto, the father of the first native Japanese nun, "found a holy relic in the food of abstinence," and presented it to Soga Umako. He proceeded to test it with

reign that is associated in subsequent history with a tremendous flowering of Buddhist art. Sometimes the period of 593–628 A.D. is called "The Suiko period" in her honor, for it witnessed the aesthetic peak of Buddhist works of art now preserved in Japan. The entire list of rulers (numbers 29– 35) from 540 to 645 A.D. was closely connected to the Soga family by blood. This "Soga dynasty" corresponds to the youthful enthusiasm of Japan for Buddhism as a mark of civilization and a protector of the state.

The connection of politics to religion and art shines through the official records. Ambitious Sogas may have truly believed in

47

such various Shamanistic-type trials as:

a) Beating it with an iron sledge, whereupon the sledge was shattered to bits, as well as the block of iron which served as an anvil.

b) Throwing the relic into water where it sank or floated on command.

Obviously Buddhism was trying to prove its "magic" was superior to that of the older *kami* or Shamanist nature spirits.

Shintoist Backlash and the Burning of Temples

Soga Umako took ill, and a diviner was called to determine the source of the disease. He said the illness sprung from a curse placed on Umako by the Buddha during the time of Soga Iname. (Perhaps destroying the image?) After this was revealed, Umako again received permission from the ruler to worship the Buddha image, but the Shintoists had other plans for this foreign religion.

Again, a pestilence was striking down hundreds in Japan. This event played right into the hands of the Mononobe and Nakatomi ceremonial chieftains. Both rebuked the Emperor for allowing the "exercise of the Buddhist religion by Soga no Omi." The Emperor vacillated between superstitious fear of the old gods (and their servants, the Shintoists) and his relatives, the Soga. Finally, he ordered Buddhism suppressed.

The Mononobe clan chief went personally to see the orders carried out, which included pulling down the temple and the pagoda, burning the images and holy books, as well as defrocking and public flogging of the high-born nuns. This was the start of a bloody feud between the Sogas on one hand and the Mononobe and Nakatomi clans on the other.

Victory of the Soga Forces and the Ascendance of Buddhism

The pot was now boiling at court, with insults traded between the two factions, as Japan geared up for what was ostensibly a religious rather than a political war. Matters were complicated for the Shintoists by the declaration made in favor of Buddhism by the Emperor Yomei (reigned 586–587 A.D., Umako's nephew, a direct-line grandson of Soga Iname).

Yomei was on his sick-bed when he made this pronouncement, and it enraged the Mononobe and Nakatomi, who proposed to ignore the orders of the Emperor. The Emperor was fading quickly; he was covered with ulcerating sores. (Smallpox was a relatively new disease in Japan.) Shiba Tatto's son vowed to leave the world and enter religion so he could intercede for the ruler's health and also to make "an image of Buddha sixteen feet high." (A "sixteen-foot high Buddha image" was a figure of speech as "sixteen" was an ideal number. The statue would not be sixteen feet tall in actual fact.)

In 587 A.D. the showdown came via a military battle. It looked like the Buddhist forces would suffer defeat. According to legend, a fifteen-year old imperial prince who later became famous as Shotoku Taishi "cut down a nuride tree and swiftly fashioned images of the Four Heavenly Kings." The prince and Soga Umako both vowed to erect temples in honor of the Four Heavenly Kings if they won the battle. Apparently this prayer was efficacious (like Constantine, who saw a vision of the Cross during battle and heard the words "by this sign you will conquer"). The Mononobe leader was defeated; he and his sons were put to death and their properties confiscated as a temple site.

Soga Umako Builds Hoko-ji

After triumphing over the Shintoist forces of the Mononobe and Nakatomi, Soga Umako kept his promise to build a grand temple for the Buddhist deities which he felt

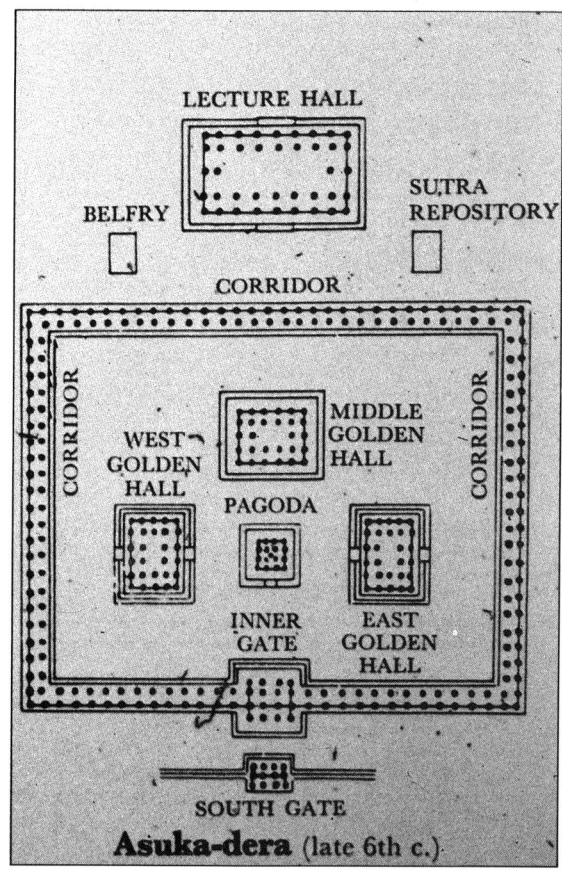

Floor plan of Hoko-ji (Asuka-dera), with three Golden Halls. It echoes such Paekche temples as Miruk-sa, which even had three pagodas, as recent excavations have discovered.

had carried the day for his clan. Since there were as yet few if any native craftsmen in Japan who understood even the basics of how to construct a Buddhist temple, the wholesale importation was needed of advisors from Paekche; they became the brains behind the operation.

Metalworkers, potters and carpenters made up the construction forces. Many of the more renowned are listed by name in the *Nihongi*, and are called *Hakase* (*paksa* in Korean), which indicates a "doctorate" in today's terminology. Twenty-two men came in the initial mission from Paekche (priests, potters, painters and others), all with one basic goal: they would build the first real temple Japan had ever seen, and in so doing reinforce the "Buddhist Party" in court politics.

The three nuns who had been publicly flogged by the Mononobe, were given into the charge of the Paekche priests Eunsol and Shyushin. The nun Aenshin, the leader of the three nuns, accompanied the priests on a trip to Paekche for study; "Horse's Child" was a careful planner.

The power of Soga Umako now increased markedly, for he could confiscate land upon a whim. The temple of Hoko-ji was built upon the site of an opponent's estate. The location was called "Asuka no Tomada"; it was central in the Horserider's city of Asuka on the Yamato Plain.

In the year of 590 A.D., the *Nihongi* recounts, with its usual penchant for brevity, that "People went to the hills to get timber for building Buddhist temples." This suggests corvée labor ordered by Soga. After assembling the giant pillars, some time elapsed in planning and construction drawings.

Hoko-ji Meant Wholesale Importation from Paekche

The Paekche craftsmen had even brought a model of a Buddha Hall with them. This Main Hall, which was to house an image of the historical Buddha, was begun in 592 A.D. The Hoko-ji temple is no longer extant, but a careful gleaning of records, plus archeological excavation reveals the basic layout and construction (see diagram). The wooden corridors enclosing a courtyard around the main Buddha Hall were completed shortly afterwards, with the pagoda constructed last. The cornerstone of the pagoda was laid in 593 A.D. with a giant pillar placed on top of a stone foundation as the central anchor.

above
Relics discovered at the base of Hoko-ji pagoda, combining both Shamanist and Buddhist symbols.
above left
Rooftiles from Hoko-ji and Wakakusa-dera (original Horyu-ji).
below left
Rooftiles from Paekche, Emileh Museum.

The pagoda was different in principles of construction than the Main Hall or outbuildings, for the pagoda's central pillar carried the weight, with the roof beams radiating outwards like a multi-stage umbrella, one of the marks of Indian nobility, from which the historical Buddha came.

When the ruins of Hoko-ji were excavated, the pagoda's foundation stone contained not what one might expect in the way of Buddhist relics, but rather many Shamanist symbols — jade *kokok*, horsebells and saddle fittings, gold and silver ornaments, and even a small model of iron armor. Buddhist relics were also included such as *sari* (the solid remains after a human body is cremated, which indicate the level of holiness achieved by the monk), buried in a small metal case. It is apparent that while the Horseriders such as the Soga clan were now becoming Buddhist, they didn't wish to offend the miscellaneous Shaman spirits of their forebears by ignoring them, so the foundation stone included the usual offerings for the dedication of an important edifice in pre-Buddhist days.

"Horse's Child" Soga Takes over Supreme Rule (592A.D.)

At the time when the covered gallery for Hoko-ji was being built, Soga Umako was disturbed by rumors that the new Soga emperor, Sujun, planned to do away with his powerful minister. Thus Umako, with his political expediency, had Sujun assassinated, and placed his own niece, Suiko, on the throne. No doubt a woman would be more

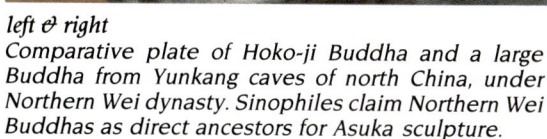

left & right
Comparative plate of Hoko-ji Buddha and a large Buddha from Yunkang caves of north China, under Northern Wei dynasty. Sinophiles claim Northern Wei Buddhas as direct ancestors for Asuka sculpture.

easily controlled, especially as it now was obvious as to what would happen to a ruler who displeased the mighty "Horse's Child."

The casting of this Buddha image commissioned by the Empress Suiko, took quite some time, for only immigrants had experience with such large metalworks. The most talented sculptor and metalworker in Japan at this time was Tori Busshi, a saddle-maker who was in favor at the court.

The nuns who had gone to Paekche for study returned, and a gala celebration occurred, combining the return of the Paekche-ordained nuns and the dedication of the main statue for Hoko-ji. Soga Umako let it be known to all that this was the Soga clan temple. He placed his son in control as nominal abbot, with priest Eji of Koguryo and Eso of Paekche as the religious heads. All the elite of Japan, headed by Empress Suiko, assembled for the ceremony of painting in the eyes of the Buddha, which were thought to make a statue "come alive" in a Buddhist sense. Soga Umako held the brush in his hand and painted the eyes in himself, for he was the most powerful man in Japan, and it was indeed his clan temple.

The *Nihongi* mentions under 605 A.D. that the king of Koguryo, having heard about the image-casting sent 300 *ryo* of gold for its gilding. This was a large amount. Japan lacked abundant silver and gold such as Korea had.

2 SHOTOKU TAISHI "THE FATHER OF JAPANESE BUDDHISM"

Shotoku's Role in the development of Japanese Buddhist culture came about slowly, but before his death in 621 A.D. he had become the premier influence on Asuka-period thought. Shotoku was an astute enough politician to know that his father-in-law, Soga Umako, would tolerate no direct rivalry in political affairs, so Shotoku busied himself with shaping Japanese society through the use of Buddhist and Confucian thought and cultural alliances with Korea; then after 607 A.D. he tried to have direct contact with China.

The historical accounts of Shotoku Taishi are filled with the stuff on legends, but all the stories emphasize his humanity and wisdom. Shotoku knew that going against the powers-that-be could mean an assassin's knife, or banishment to a distant, barbarous area. His birth is described as miraculous in a way, for his mother was delivered of him without effort at the door of the horse stables. (The symbolism of horses was still very strong in early Buddhist Japan.)

The scholastic upbringing of Shotoku was remarkable for he learned both Confucian and Buddhist thought from his Korean tutors. This allowed him to be an authority on sacred (Buddhist) and secular legal matters.

Shotoku and Buddhist Culture

In 595 A.D. a Koguryo priest named Hyecha arrived; he was to become the Prince Imperial's teacher and greatly influenced this heir to the Japanese throne. The year before, Shotoku had begun the construction of Shitenno-ji (Four Heavenly Kings' Temple), and aloe wood was first used to make incense.

Portrait of Shotoku Taishi and his two sons, traditionally attributed to the hand of Crown Prince Asa of Paekche (Imperial Household Collection)

In 601 A.D. Shotoku began building his Ikaruga Palace; it was very close to where the second Horyu-ji now stands. Shotoku also personally oversaw the making of "shields and banners" with Buddhist themes, as well as giving out Buddhist images to those nobles who wished to convert to the new faith.

One of Shotoku's most notable achievements was a seventeen-part doctrine somewhat like a constitution, but which governed moral and civil conduct. His devotion to Buddhism can be seen, for the entire second clause deals with its "Three Treasures" and commands the reverence of Buddhist teachings as a way to achieve personal goodness and proper conduct.

Aerial view of Horyu-ji, built after 670 A.D., located just north of Shotoku's original temple of Wakakusa-dera ("The first Horyu-ji" of 607 A.D.)

Shotoku's Favorite Temple: Horyu-ji

As a youth, Shotoku had participated, with his aunt, Empress Suiko, in all the ceremonies connected with the erection of Hoko-ji, Japan's first major Buddhist temple and the Soga clan's own edifice. Although a member of this clan, and son-in-law of the mighty Soga Umako, still as Shotoku progressed further in his scholarly studies, he wished to erect a temple of his own, or one which he and his aunt could share, just as they shared civil authority. (There is no record that Shotoku and his aunt-empress ever quarreled.)

In 601 the Ikaruga Palace was built for the Prince Imperial; his aunt's old "palace" had a leaky roof. (The first mention of a palace having a tile roof is 643 A.D.) Adjacent to the new palace, Shotoku erected his Buddhist temple, employing Paekche workmen. It became the prince-regent's personal devotional center, and appears to be where he studied sutras with the Koguryo priest Hye-cha. The temple also housed personnel who practiced medicine, for new medical knowledge was one of the benefits of Buddhist importation. Adjacent dormitories housed student-monks and teacher-monks.

Shotoku's personal temple was first called Wakakusa-dera. Many of the famous sculptural pieces, now "National Treasures" in Horyu-ji, were initially in this older, somewhat smaller temple, some yards south of the present site. When Soga Iruka decided to exterminate all of Shotoku's descendants, he ordered Ikaruga Palace burned, and the family of Shotoku killed, but Iruka left the temple built by Shotoku strictly alone — perhaps out of superstitious fear. Thus, Wakakusa-dera survived, until, as recorded in the *Nihongi* under the year 670 A.D.:

> After midnight, a fire broke out in Horiu-ji. (sic) Not a single building was left.

Since a thunderstorm also occurred that night, the fire may have begun from a lightning bolt, the tall pagoda being struck first. If the pagoda burned first, this allowed the monks time to remove the major pieces of art from the Golden Hall next door. Thus a few major icons of Asuka art still remain. These icons testify in a remarkable way to the skill of Korean artists.

Master Builders from Paekche

The *Nihongi* records numerous master craftsmen coming from Paekche to assist in building the first Soga temple. After it was completed, the architects were free to build other temples and palaces.

Shotoku's mansion was completed by the end of 605; the first Horyu-ji is dated 607 A.D. Since the original Horyu-ji burned in 670, its architecture must be judged by the second Horyu-ji. Buddhist art, being a hallowed tradition, discouraged architects from tampering with basic design, especially something as difficult as a pagoda. Therefore, when looking at Horyu-ji, the buildings differ mainly in overall size and small details from the ones built by Shotoku Taishi.

Furthermore, when Horyu-ji burned in

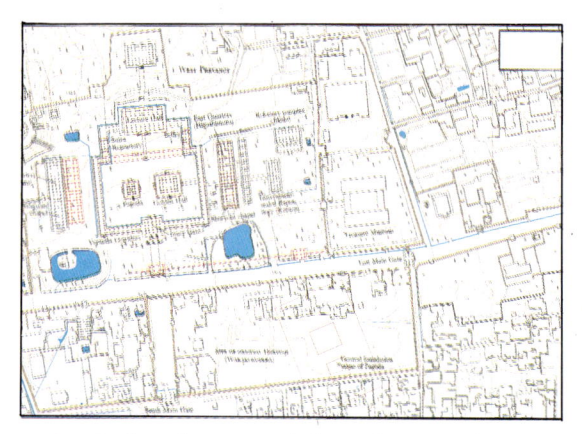

Ground plan showing Wakakusa-dera in relation to the extant temple of Horyu-ji.

670, the Soga clan was out of power, and its enemies held the throne. In fact, Emperor Temmu, who ascended the throne in 672 A.D., had personally dispatched the last of the powerful Sogas. It was a tribute to Shotoku himself that Horyu-ji was rebuilt. His family line had been exterminated, but his reputation as a Buddhist saint had grown. So the new clan, the anti-Soga party, allocated the money to rebuild Shotoku's temple.

Horyu-ji's rebuilding took some years, because only so much money at a time would be appropriated by the new line of rulers. However, they could not totally ignore the project, and skilled artisans from abroad were now plentiful.

Many Paekche workmen who were refugees from the fall of their kingdom, may have felt that Horyu-ji stood not only as a monument to Shotoku, but to their ability as artist-artisans of now-vanished Paekche.

Horyu-ji Pagoda: Paekche Masterpiece

Even though Shotoku and Empress Suiko were dead, the major figures of the Soga line killed, and the pro-Shintoists in control, it would have been unthinkable not to employ the best artisans for Horyu-ji's reconstruction; they would be skilled immigrants from Paekche. No copy is quite like the original, thus the second Horyu-ji reflects mainly changes in Paekche style between 600–660 A.D.

The early type of "cloud brackets" which shows so clearly on the Tamamushi Shrine, reflecting slightly earlier Paekche architecture, has been somewhat changed, as has the arrangement. One custom that apparently did not change was the anchoring system for a wooden pagoda. No one can be sure how or when this method developed, or if the design owes something to the structure of an umbrella, a favorite motif in Indian architecture. However, stone and metal umbrella shapes would be quite different from wooden ones.

The centerpost of the pagoda was an octagonal wooden post, sunk into the ground about ten feet, and anchored to a foundation

opposite page & above
Comparative plate of roofline silhouettes, a stone Paekche pagoda in Puyo, Korea and a wooden Paekche pagoda in Japan (Horyu-ji)

Hokki-ji pagoda, contemporary with nearby Horyu-ji, showing Paekche-type construction.

stone at the base. According to the *Samguk Yusa,* Paekche architects were commissioned by Silla to erect its tallest wooden pagoda, surpassing 224 feet, consisting of nine stories. Horyu-ji's pagoda, now stands 108 feet tall. Silla's attempt at monumental architecture in wood was completed in 643 A.D. (and rebuilt after each succeeding fire).

The 660 A.D. defeat of Paekche proved a very fortuitous event for the development of Japanese architecture. There are those enthusiasts who believe that the 130-feet high Yakushi-ji pagodas were supervised and constructed by Paekche-trained architects. This may be correct. At the very least, one can conservatively state that the present Horyu-ji pagoda is a prime example of seventh-century Paekche temple architecture. It should be included in the catalogs of Korean art as "Paekche," much in the same way that Koryo celadon in the Metropolitan Museum is labeled "Korean."

Two smaller temples, also associated with Horyu-ji, had three-story pagodas built by Paekche workmen. These buildings follow the design of the Horyu-ji pagoda closely, except in parameters of size. Hokki-ji was finished in 685 A.D., so it may have employed craftsmen who worked on the second Horyu-ji. The same may be said for Horin-ji, a small, nearby temple with a very similar pagoda.

Asuka had been the hometown for the

Horseriders. Under Buddhist influence it next became a center for Korean art and architecture. Only when the capital of Japan moved to Nara, in 710 A.D., did the major religious edifices begin to become slavishly Chinese.

Horyu-ji may seem small compared with Miruk-sa, the largest Paekche temple compound built. However, Japan's most famous pagoda, 21 feet square on a side and 108 feet tall, and its adjacent Golden Hall, measuring 47 by 36 feet, are truly excellent examples of Paekche wooden-style art and architecture, none are remaining in Korea.

Korean Nobility

When the "new line" came to the throne in 646 A.D. by murdering the Soga leader, this was not an anti-Korean move. Almost all of Japan's nobility, if traced back far enough, had come from the continent, largely from Korea. Even the Nakatomi, leaders of the Shinto religion, had ancestors who were simply earlier immigrants from Korea than the Horseriders' line. Some Koreans became naturalized immediately; a few held on to their ancestral names for a generation or so. The semi-Korean court granted ranks of nobility, landed estates and positions of trust to these newcomers. In fact, when the first census (*Seishi-roku*) to survive came out in 814 A.D., about one-third of the nobility could trace their families to Korean or Chinese ancestors. Some of the Chinese tended to return home after a period of years teaching various arts, but the Koreans more frequently remained because of civil disturbances in their own country, and because they were so richly rewarded in Japan.

In this early peerage census, 162 families registered as from various provinces in China and 172 from Korea. Of these, the largest proportion (104) was from Paekche. Of course, many non-nobles formed the craftsmen and skilled laborers. Textile mak-

Stone garden ornament representing the Buddhist "World Mountain," Sumeru. A Paekche refugee built Japan's first formal garden in 612 A.D. Soga Umako's pond-and-island garden became so famous that he was nicknamed "Lord of the Garden Isle."

ing seems to have been largely derived from Korea.

Music and dancing instructors from Korea were manifestly popular. The first mentioned came in 612 A.D., and Korean dances remained in demand at the court. The carving of masks for dramatic performances was in Korean hands. Gardening seems to have been largely a preserve of skilled Koreans in the early days.

From the names of some of the early temples, such as "Paekche Temple" (Kudara-dera) and "Koguryo Temple" (Koma-dera), it would seem that the newcomers first worshipped at their special temples, and later began to mix with the populace at large. Japan was the land of opportunity; special skills which were middle class livelihoods in Korea, often rated a peerage in Japan. No prejudice existed, but rather a welcome mat for immigrants from a superior civilization.

Paekche Kuanyin, Called "Kudara Kannon" in Japan (ht. 209.4 cm., 82 in.)

Throughout the thirty-six years when Japan ruled Korea as a colony, the official line was that the peninsula's history and culture were inferior to those of the island empire. However, one ancient wooden statue of Horyu-ji did not lose its popular name of "Kudara Kannon," which means "Paekche Kuanyin," in spite of the general attitude. To have the name persist indicates some special quality about this work of art. It deserves to be studied carefully.

This very tall wooden statue formerly stood on the dais of the Golden Hall at Horyu-ji, Shotoku's personal temple. The statue was moved to a glass case in that temple's Treasure Museum for safekeeping after a 1949 fire destroyed part of the Golden Hall. Due to reflective glass used in the museum case, it is difficult to appreciate the real grace of this statue. It is better studied via photographs than in actuality. (The famous Laurence Binyon ordered a replica for London's British Museum and Tokyo National Museum also has an exact copy, minus glass).

This graceful figure, with an almost tender expression on its face, clearly calls out its artistic origins in the traditions of the most genteel of Korea's Three Kingdoms. From the openwork crown, which still rests on the forehead down to the design of the lotus petals at the bottom, the marks of early seventh-century Paekche workmanship are all about it. Possibly this personification of the Buddhist concept of mercy or compassion could have been chiseled from a medium-sized

Full-length photo of Horyu-ji's Paekche Kuanyin, for centuries called "Kudara Kannon" by Japanese admirers.

camphor tree in Japan. However, the sculptors of this masterpiece certainly were not fumble-figured or unfamiliar with the techniques of Paekche and the softened lines which characterize its Buddhist images.

When focusing attention on this work of art, it becomes apparent just how far some Japanese art critics have gone to cast doubt on Paekche's influence and craftsmanship during Asuka period. (They even date this statue considerably later to make it seem more reasonable as the work of a Japanese artist.)

To quote the late Professor Seiichi Mizuno, a time-honored scholar of Chinese sculpture (and therefore an authority on Horyu-ji):

> It is difficult to abandon the now firmly entrenched name of 'Kudara Kannon'...The materials — camphor for the statue itself and cypress for the platform and phial the statue holds — clearly indicate that the work was made in Japan.

However, Korea has tall *Cinnamun camphora*. This is the Latin name for camphor trees. Mizuno was wrong. The Arboretum at Chollipo, considerably north of the old Paekche capital cities, grows camphor trees. Instead of the species of wood, it is more informative to really examine the style, without a mental set. Most of Mizuno's life was lived during the colonial period (1910–45) when the phrase was coined "not worth a Kudara."

Bronze Jewelry

The first and foremost clue, which clearly indicates Paekche handiwork, is the crown's design (See diagram) which shows the characteristic honeysuckle-lotus pattern found in artifacts buried in the tomb of Paekche's King Munyong (reigned 501–523 A.D.). The number of protrusions from the petals is identical. The coiling of the vines appears the same. Crowns of nearly identical type remain in Korea, executed in both gilt bronze and granite.

This wooden statue's crown and the Dream Hall figure both have lapis-like jewel ornaments. Above the central jewel is a tiny, engraved image, an Amitabha, part of the iconography for a Kuanyin.

The crown's pendants indicate a carryover from Shamanist designs seen in fifth-century

Jewelry on the Paekche Kuanyin, Horyu-ji's Treasure Museum.

Korean crowns. All Korean crowns of that period so far discovered have such accessory side pieces, the meaning of which is a moot point. Buddhist artists could adopt Shamanist motifs and change the meaning slightly to suit their purposes. The older motifs have simply become "Buddhacized," but the skills and techniques built up in Korean metalwork over a period of several centuries could not be duplicated so quickly by a new art tradition. This type of metalwork never did emerge in Japan. After Paekche artisans ceased to be a dominant factor, such crowns, etc. disappeared. Throughout history Japan is known as a "copyist" who borrows and later assimilates, choosing what suits the islanders best. As long as the patrons for

Buddhist art in Japan were all Korean-descended, artists lacked encouragement to develop other styles. As long as Paekche workmen were fleeing their own country, there was no need to develop a separate Japanese Buddhist art tradition.

Kuanyin's bronze bracelets and those of the wooden Four Heavenly Kings, who still stand guard at the four corners of the dais in the center of Horyu-ji's Golden Hall, evidence quite similar openwork designs. Some Sinophile critics of Japan have labeled this "filigree," but it is not true filigree. To make such bracelets, for example, the artisan first made a flat sheet of bronze, and then laid it on an iron block. Patterns were cut into the sheet with iron chisels, and then it was put on a gradated wooden stick and bent into an oval shape. After this, the bracelet-in-the-making was slipped over the wrist. It was moved to the desired position, closed, and hammered together, being fixed in place with metal pins inserted into pre-cut holes in the bronze.

Mandorla

The Paekche Kuanyin's wooden mandorla was slightly carved and then painted with lacquer colors. It has not been retouched, so is now quite faded. This halo has three separate and distinct circles, each with a different design. The outer section is not completely circular, but rises upwards to a point of "heavenly fire," a shape which can be seen in modern Kirilan photographs of a human being's aura.

The very center point of the three circles contains a lotus, the holy flower of Buddhism. The teachings of Buddhism designate the lotus as a symbol of the human ability to rise above craving and desire, in the way that a lotus rises from the odious slime and mud at the bottom of a stagnant pond to burst forth into bloom above the scum which floats upon

Detail showing Paekche Kuanyin's mandorla, Horyu-ji's Treasure Museum.

the pond's surface (the ordinariness of life). This lotus displays the same soft edges and somewhat flattened surface which characterize the Paekche rooftiles now surviving and on exhibit in Korean museums.

The smallest circle of the mandorla's pattern of three rings is faded; the second has a twisting lotus leaf and vine motif, and the last layer is "filled with a jewel design" according to Mizuno. He claims to have often encountered the same thing in Chinese Buddhist art of the Sui period (590–618 A.D.). At present only peeling or flaking paint shows here, but since Professor Mizuno, like a host of others, sees Chinese art styles in Asuka objects (without reference to Korean influence), one must assume that these motifs came from China to Japan via a "flying carpet," since no

Closeup of Paekche Kuanyin's face, Horyu-ji's Treasure Museum.

boats were then plying directly through the waves which separated the two countries.

For this peak period of Buddhist art now kept in Japan, there is absolutely no record of any Chinese Buddha images coming to the islands, either small bronzes, stone or wooden images. No Japanese artist or artists are recorded as visiting China at this time. But a number of both images and skilled artisans are recorded coming from Korea. They also had not traveled to China. "Flying carpet" is the answer!

Paekche Grace on the Face

Paekche characteristics, such as softened facial lines (as opposed to Koguryo's sharper edges) are well displayed in the features of this wooden "Kudara Kannon" which has been in Japan at Horyu-ji so many centuries. The sensual nature of the brow's curve displays an other-worldly quality, as though the being represented had one foot in the real world and the other in the celestial spheres. Although not quite smiling, the viewer is reminded of the "Paekche smile" seen in earlier stone sculpture still in place in Korea.

In this wooden artifact, the nose bears the characteristic high bridge and accentuated nostril curve found on so many other Paekche-influenced Asuka works. Later examples of Korean Buddhist art show the same ethereal quality, especially in the portrayal of angels in bronze.

If the "Kudara Kannon" icon had been afforded the same protection from the elements as the Dream Hall Kuanyin received, then this Paekche treasure of wood carving might be even more incredibly beautiful. Even so, it may be called the finest example of Paekche sculpture in the medium of wood to have survived (in the entire world). It is understandable that the ancient name has still been retained, in spite of racial discrimination.

To Stand upon a Lotus

The cypress wood pedestal, carved with down-turned lotus leaves, is somewhat unique because of its double-veined petal motif. This mannerism is neither Sui-period Chinese nor Wei-period Chinese. Also the softness of the petals separates it from Koguryo styles, which are harder (seemingly sharp enough to cut the hand that touches them).

The petals seem to flow outward from the feet, almost like water from a basin, or the sheerest silk. Sensual lines these; all the lines of this sculpture flow with continuity, like the turning of the Buddhist Wheel of the Law. This testifies to the whole-hearted faith

left & right
Frontal view and details showing the Paekche Kuanyin's left hand holding the holy water bottle. Horyu-ji's Treasure Museum.

of Paekche's tradition.

Melodious Hands

After the Asuka period, when Korean craftsmanship became much less marked, the skill required to produce a spiritual image carved from one piece of wood almost totally disappeared. Practicality took the place of difficulty and various parts of the body were joined or doweled into the main trunk, which might itself be cut from several pieces. A carved sash or some other part of the costume covered up the places were the pieces joined. The skill of monolithic carving finds its apex in the Horyu-ji pieces. (What may have once existed on the Korean peninsula has been burned; it can only be surmised from Horyu-ji's Asuka-period "National Treasures," when Asuka was still a settlement dominated by Koreans.)

The Paekche Kuanyin now preserved in Horyu-ji's Treasure Museum, can be seen to hold a vessel in its left hand. This vessel has changed in metaphorical meaning as Mahayana Buddhism developed. The basic shape of this water bottle began as one of three essential items which an Indian monk needed for life in this material world, after he had renounced "craving" — namely, a patched robe, a begging bowl and a water bottle. (The begging bowl was to become gilded, the robe a pattern of richly embroidered silks and the water bottle gained a second spout). The bottle changed the least as converts traveled across the Silk Route into

61

above
Full-length view of Dream Hall Kuanyin statue, called "Yumedono Kannon" in Japan, Horyu-ji's Dream Hall.

China and the Buddhist religion evolved into a vast system to satisfy millions. In Korea the water bottle evolved into the beautifully curvaceous *kundika* of Koryo-period celadons. Tantric Buddhism used the *kundika* shape for a baptismal ceremony, the supplicant's head being sprinkled with magical holy water in an "elevation" ritual.

Here at Horyu-ji the bottle retains a seventh-century shape, which was repeated with regularity up to the present day in Korean Buddhist sculptures showing Kuanyin.

The downward-turned hands of Horyu-ji's "Kudara Kannon" show the curved, yet jointed fingers characteristic of Paekche art. This tendency in rendering the shape of the digits clearly differentiates Paekche sculpture from Koguryo and Silla. In their works, the curve of the fingers became more important than showing the flexion of a joint. Koguryo tomb paintings, as well as most of the statuary, contain fingers which appear to have no more body or shape than a piece of over-cooked macaroni, or a frankfurter bent into a funny shape. (The Paekche Kuanyin's hands and fingers remind a Western art historian of thirteenth-century Byzantine Virgin's hands.)

The most abiding characteristic of the Paekche Kuanyin's hands is the conveying of a gentle strength, firm yet supple — melody in wood. The right hand is outstretched in a beckoning posture, calling the supplicant forward to unload the pain felt within. The complete effect is that of the craftsman's original intent, the embodiment of mercy, beckoning towards the path of righteousness, all accomplished within a single tree trunk!

The "Dream Hall Kuanyin" (Yumedono Kannon)

Not a single piece of wooden sculpture remains on the Korean peninsula from the period which saw its fluorescence, namely the early seventh century. During civil wars, wooden buildings and sculptural pieces carved from wood are totally vulnerable to fire. However by a fortuitous circumstance, examples of Korean skills at this time do remain in Japan, clustered around Shotoku Taishi's temple of Horyu-ji.

Hye-cha of Koguryo as an Important Influence

One statue has a long and complex history and received extraordinary veneration for centuries. Putting together pieces of evidence, most of them recorded in the *Nihongi* as memorable events, it is known that on the tenth day in the fifth month of the year 595 A.D., a remarkable Koguryo priest named Hye-cha emigrated to the Japanese court located at Asuka. Apparently he came on request, for he "was taken as a teacher by the Prince Imperial" Shotoku Taishi. The teacher-disciple relationship lasted a long time and the two became very close. Although he studied the Confucian classics, Shotoku's special interest was Buddhism. He learned to read Chinese, the only written language that Japan then possessed, and gave lectures to the Asuka court on the meaning of various sutras. Presumably he had first studied these holy books with Priest Hye-cha of Koguryo.

With Hye-cha's help, this studious crown prince, who was serving as regent for his aunt, the Empress Suiko, became the main patron of several major Buddhist temples. Decorative accessories such as banners and embroideries made the interiors splendid, along with wooden statues. Bronze casting was still difficult to accomplish in Japan, and bronze statues were used only for special temples. However, when a wooden statue was gilded with paint or covered with gold leaf, ordinary people could not tell the difference.

Since Hye-cha came from Koguryo, he knew more about China, especially the unification process that was taking place there under the Sui-dynasty leaders. It may have been Hye-cha who urged the Prince-Regent Shotoku to reach beyond Korea and open direct communications with the new Sui rulers of a somewhat unified China. Shotoku did dispatch envoys in 607 A.D., all of them being of Korean descent who could read Chinese; the boat coasted the Korean shoreline as a direct passage was too dangerous. Ancient records report that the Chief Envoy (a Korean) asked the Chinese emperor to address Japan as "Land of the Sun" instead of "Land of Dwarfs," but this was not done until 670 A.D. (again at the suggestion of a Korean, who felt the term insulted Japan).

This first mission to China returned within a year, and doesn't seem to have accomplished too much. There is no record of Buddhist statues being sent as part of the exchange of "gifts" from ruler to ruler. The art works, those recorded, all came from one of the three kingdoms of Korea. Presumably most of these Buddhist statues and holy books or banners came privately, some going to Kyushu, and were not included in the *Nihongi*. In a centralized country such as the young Japan, power and influence on art spread outward from the capital of Asuka.

At length towards the end of the year 615 A.D., the now-aging Koguryo Buddhist priest Hye-cha decided to return to his homeland. His mission to educate the next ruler, plus his aunt the present ruler, had been accomplished. During the two decades that Hye-cha was present in Asuka, the Buddhist coloration of the court elite had become noticeable. Temples, especially under Soga clan patronage, were springing up in many localities.

Hye-cha's Strong Reaction to Shotoku's Death

In 621 A.D. when Shotoku's Buddhist teacher-confidant Hye-cha heard of the unexpected death in his sleep of Shotoku, on the fifth day of the second month of spring, he felt deep grief. This was a blow for Buddhism's cause in Japan. He needed to prolong its prestige by using Shotoku's death as meaningful — rather than just a sudden tragedy. The *Nihongi* states:

At this time Hye-cha, the Buddhist priest of Koguryo, heard of the death of the Prince Imperial and was greatly grieved thereat. He invited the priests, and in honor of the Prince Imperial gave them a (vegetarian) meal saying:

"In the land of Nippon there is a sage. —I, although a foreigner was in heart closely united to him. Now what avails it that I alone should survive? I have determined to die on the fifth day of the second month of next year. So I shall meet the Prince Imperial in the Pure Land...."

At this time, a memorial service was held on the first anniversary of death, and Hye-cha died on that day, as he had prophesied.

Although the *Nihongi* does not record it, it was the custom to present gifts on memorial funerals. Hye-cha seems to have moved quickly. An order was placed for a statue "in the image of Prince Shotoku." A temple had been built in 607 A.D. First called Wakakusadera, it is now referred to as "the first Horyu-ji." This was the personal temple of Shotoku and his aunt, Empress Suiko. It had become a scholarly center for Shotoku. What better memorial for Hye-cha to give for the first anniversary than a wooden statue, ordered gilded to look like bronze? Probably this statue was first placed in Shotoku's temple, and when it burned in 670 A.D. was rescued by faithful monks.

Shotoku's "Dream Hall" Built

Admirers of Prince Shotoku, apparently on the hundredth anniversary of his death, built an octagonal wooden pavilion, in the shape of a Korean pavilion, and the statue carved in memorium to him was placed inside this pavilion, known today as "The Dream Hall." It was intended as a memorial to Shotoku, to "give him pleasant dreams" in the Pure Land. As the central statue of this Dream Hall, the most appropriate icon was the gilded

Octagonal sanctuary termed the Dream Hall, built in the mid-eighth century in memorium for Shotoku Taishi. This building houses the Dream Hall Kuanyin wooden statue, which became "sacred" or "forbidden."

wooden one made "in the image of Shotoku," and also associated with his teacher, Priest Hye-cha of Koguryo.

No other statue of this early period has received such honors as to be made "a forbidden image" not to be seen by ordinary human eyes. For centuries it was "sacred" and worshipped in its black lacquer case without being opened and unwrapped. No other piece of Asuka-period art received such reverence.

Forbidden Image Associated with Two "Sages"?

The explanation would seem to lie in the fact that this statue now in the Dream Hall (presently seen only one day a year, even in modern times) was associated with *two* sages. The *Nihongi* provides an explanation. It recounts that Hye-cha did die on the exact first anniversary of Shotoku's death, as he had prophesied. People then said, according to the *Nihongi*:

The Prince is not the only sage. Hye-cha is also a sage.

64

Thus there were two "saints" to be honored with the worship of this wooden statue. One was a Korean Buddhist priest from Koguryo and the other is known as "Shotoku, the Father of Japanese Buddhism." His bloodline was Korean, but his ancestors had been living in Japan for two centuries, since his family, the Soga, stemmed from the "Valiant Old Bear Lord" who helped Jingu with the 369 A.D. invasion.

This statue called the "Dream Hall Kuanyin" or *Yumedono Kannon* in Japanese, received reverence which was unique in Japan. It might still be enshrouded in its yards and yards of silk. However, after Commodore Perry forced Japan out of its shell, as a part of Japan's desire for rapid progress in Westernization, traditional art lessened in value almost to the zero point. (At this time American museums such as the Boston Museum of Art and the Freer Gallery were able to purchase many of the masterpieces that they now hold.) An American, Ernest Fenollosa, had become an enthusiast of Japan's traditional arts, particularly Buddhist pieces.

The Japanese government recognized his stance and appointed him as a sort of official inspector to go around and study such things as ancient temple art. At that time, the 1870s, Buddhist temples were in bad repair, many of them. The Tokugawa Shogunate had downplayed the power of Buddhism and thus many abbots were really only census-keepers for the dictatorial government. Then, with 1868, the Meiji government began to stress and build up State Shintoism. The repute of Japan's Buddhist art had fallen to an all-time low.

Armed with his official credentials, Fenollosa, later to become Curator of the Boston Museum of Art, (accompanied by Okakura Tenshin, later Japan's most famous painter) demanded to see the "sacred statue" preserved in Shotoku's Dream Hall on the site of

The Dream Hall Kuanyin's serene expression which greeted Fenollosa upon completion of the statue's momentous unwrapping.

his seventh-century Ikaruga Palace. Shotoku's "dreams" were to be interrupted!

"Korean, of Course"

When the first unwrapping of this "holy icon" started, after its many centuries long dormant period, peals of thunder filled the air. (Thunder is relatively rare in the Yamato region.) This frightened Horyu-ji's superstitious monks. However, Ernest Fenollosa was not to be stopped. Eventually the entire wooden image was unwrapped from its silk yardage, and exposed to the light of day for the first time in well over half a millennium. His diary records that, on seeing the entire wooden statue, Fenollosa remarked to Okakura, "Korean, of course." In those days, before the Sino-Japanese War, before the Russo-Japanese War, when Japan's colonial ambitions towards Korea had not yet formalized, to say an art piece was "Korean" was not using a dirty word.

But is this statue "Korean," as Fenollosa so quickly surmised? In those days, the art historian had not himself seen much Korean art. Fenollosa was later to write "Epochs of Chinese and Japanese Art," which became the standard English language art history for the Far East during the 1920s and 1930s of this century. Apparently Fenollosa felt that the statue was not "Japanese" and not "Chinese," and knowing the great influence of Korea on the Asuka-based kingdom, reached the only reasonable conclusion.

Viewing this statue from an objective point of view, what is apparent? The actual icon stands 1.805 meters high, or a little short of six feet. According to tradition, these measurements are those of Shotoku himself. The average height of Japanese men in Fenollosa's lifetime was about five foot three inches, but Shotoku's bloodline came from the Horseriders, from northern stock which was much taller than the average Japanese.

The gold leaf covering this wood carving is better preserved than for any other seventh-century statue in Japan, but this is to be expected due to its careful storage and preservation from the light of day for so many centuries as a "holy image."

What made Fenollosa exclaim, "Korean, of course"? Was it because of the artifact's two dimensional quality, its flatness, its "fins" or sawtooth-cutouts along the outer edges of the robe, a technique or mannerism begun by Wei-dynasty bronze casters? (Wei wooden images have totally disappeared; did such a mannerism exist in their wooden art?) Did this artifice occur because the carver wished to give more three-dimensionality to his statue's appearance, but was limited by the monolithic log of wood which was his material? (Monolithic wooden sculpture was largely given up in Japan after the Korean influence waned, as it is a difficult technique indeed!)

above
Detail showing the intricate openwork design of the gilt bronze crown belonging to the Dream Hall Kuanyin.
opposite page
Closeup of the brow and facial lines of the Dream Hall Kuanyin, revealing Koguryo influence.

The Orient's Most Elaborate Bronze Crown

The wooden statue known as the Dream Hall Kuanyin possesses the most intricate bronze crown of any statue in Asia. It appears to be a mixture of several styles (all Korean) and designs; no known parallel exists with purely Japanese workmanship. Crowns found to date by archeologists within Japan can only be classed as poor country cousins to this painstakingly-wrought bronze creation. Evidently it was shaped and cut out by a master craftsman, someone having a long tradition of metal technology behind him. The basic design was drawn from the tradition of the Horseriders, as evidenced by their objects in iron, bronze and gilt-bronze. Koguryo tomb painting also has similar designs, such as the "climbing flame," and the eagle with outstretched wings, plus a slightly modified honeysuckle pattern.

The crown bears jewels of several types, the most noticeable being the lapis-like blue globes. These outline the figure of a human being in their placement. At the pinnacle of the crown stand onion-dome type cutouts, pieces which take the shape of the sacred fire of Buddhism. (This motif is shared by both Koguryo and Paekche.)

Just as the fifth-century crowns found in Kyongju tombs all have pendants on each side, so the crown of the Dream Hall Kuanyin originally had pendants hanging from each side. The one on the left of the head is still preserved, but the one that should fall over the Kuanyin's right chest is missing. Apparently this statue was not made "sacred" in its seventh-century beginnings, but later. Perhaps after slight damage had been noticed, it was sealed away before more than one pendant was missing. Later authorities must have recognized that such intricate bronze work could not be easily duplicated. Thus, at some unknown time, the wooden statue was made "secret."

Brow and Eyeline Reflect Koguryo and Paekche

Perhaps the most noticeable characteristic of the facial lines which grace this Dream

Hall Kuanyin is the softness of the brow ridge. It merges as naturally as possible into the forehead, as those of a life-like living person. This, which can be termed "the Paekche brow," shows how Paekche and Koguryo had become blended in their artistic styles by the year 600 A.D.

The drape of the religious robes shows stiff folds with sharp edges, but the eyes reveal the softening that underscores the cheek lines and brow ridges. This appeared particularly in sculpture south of the Han River, in Paekche territory, before unification of the peninsula.

Legends from antiquity hold that the face of this Dream Hall Kuanyin represents that of Shotoku Taishi. The work itself is said to have been in memorium of him and thus to represent the prince. The high-bridged nose and high cheek bones both suggest continental origin for the sculptor's model; they definitely indicate the Korean heritage of the Soga clan, to which Shotoku belonged. (Divergence can be seen when the Dream Hall statue and Asuka art in general are compared with later, purely native Japanese art. Those sculptured figures have a flatter set of nostrils with a sometimes very low bridge to the nose.)

The same shape of the eyes can still be seen in Korean sculpture of the Koryo period. The Korean eye and brow ridge together were to continue through Unified Silla, even though the body proportions lost their graceful, Wei-influenced or Sui-influenced lines, and become the chubby-cheeked Buddhas and bodhisattvas which indicate T'ang-period Chinese influence. Such plump appearance suggests the affluence of Unified Silla's elite society. However, the ethereal, other-worldly quality which characterizes the face of this Dream Hall Kuanyin disappears from both Japanese and Korean art shortly after the seventh century.

Koguryo Scrollwork on Painted Mandorla

More than fifty tombs remain from Koguryo's fourth to its seventh century, which are decorated with paintings on their granite walls or ceiling slabs. These patterns show some similarities to China's Han-dynasty tombs as far as using the four directional animals for their major subject matter on the four sides. Also a motif termed a "honeysuckle leaf" occurs over and over. The center of its two outward curving leaves may be a three-petaled, blossoming lotus thrusting upwards. This same feature is repeated in the second circle of the mandorla behind the Dream Hall Kuanyin.

Another type of decoration, this one on the outer circle, can be termed Koguryo's "climbing flame design." Initially this motif is found in Han-dynasty Chinese lacquer work. Very few bronze pieces survive from the royal tombs which dot the plain of the Taedong River and stretch forth to the Yalu River and on to Manchuria. However, one gilt-bronze cap has been preserved; it matches this wall design. This bronze artifact (See illustration) has both a phoenix and a three-legged crow, with the sinuous patterns of its body construction forming designs of continuity. One gilt-bronze Koguryo crown from the fifth century also survives, to reveal the same type of design. Apparently this particular motif held deep meaning for the North Korean Shamanist as well as the later Buddhists of the Koguryo kingdom.

"Little Sister" of the Dream Hall Kuanyin

A number of small bronze statuettes came to Japan, probably in the voluminous sleeves of traveling priests. Devotional images of one type or another were considered appropriate "gifts" from official and private persons traveling from Korea to the culture-conscious court of Asuka Japan. These tiny images were in bronze, rather than wood, but the ar-

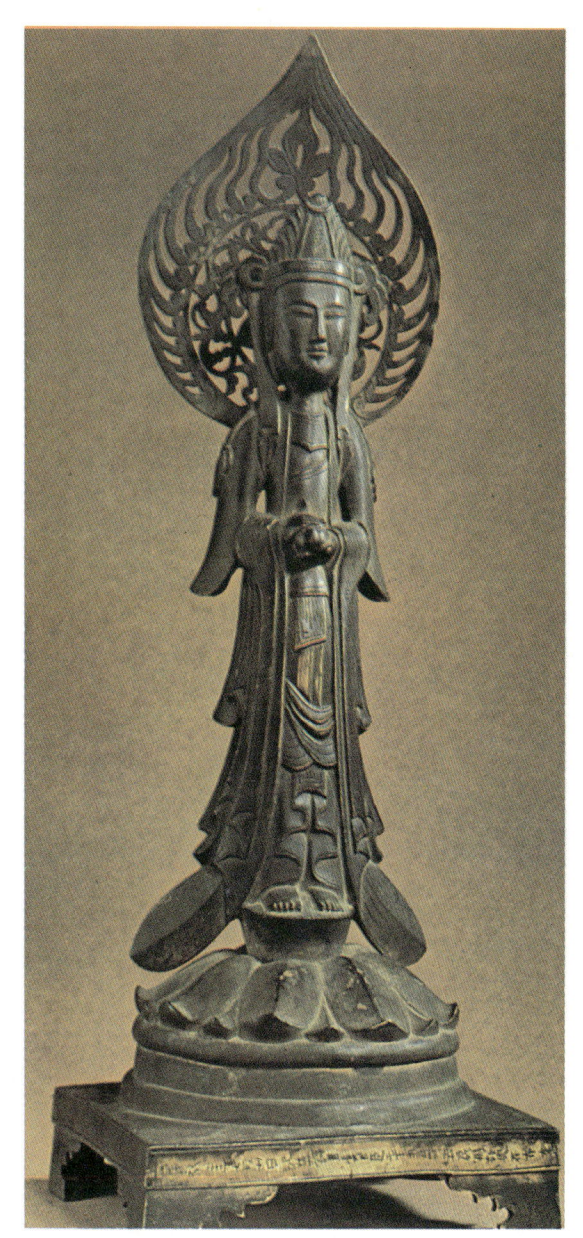

top left & middle left
Comparative plate with detail of Dream Hall Kuanyin's mandorla with honeysuckle and lotus design and a 7th-century Koguryo tomb mural with a very similar pattern.
right & bottom left
"Little Sister" of the Dream Hall Kuanyin statue, Tokyo National Museum (originally kept at Horyu-ji). This rock-cut Paekche sculpture is in South Chungchong Province.

69

tistic roots and iconography were very similar.

A climbing flame pattern is found in their halos as well as their mandorlas. One in particular, illustrated here, seems to be a "little sister" to the Dream Hall Kuanyin, only different because of size. The extreme frontality is present, and the somewhat sharpened lines of the face. Both bear a Koguryo stamp. The interior circle of the tiny halo also holds the honeysuckle pattern, a continuance of Shamanist design carried over into Buddhism.

The crown which rests on the head of this "Little Sister" is similar to that of the larger figure, but the nature of the lost wax casting technique prevents the rendering of as many details in the small tiara. Both have a high front piece with two smaller side wings. The dangling trains which descend earthward are not as carefully stylized in the small bronze, but this is due to the size.

This petite statuette (29cm.) has a lotus pedestal base which possesses "cutting edge" promontories on the petals. Koguryo sculptors inherited this mannerism from Northern Wei, and carried it almost to extremes at times. Paekche softened the edges, flattening the petals completely in most cases.

The hand position (holding the wishing jewel in precisely the same way as the Dream Hall Kuanyin) establishes a unique relationship, not duplicated elsewhere in Asuka art. Could this miniature bronze statuette have once belonged to Koguryo priest Hye-cha, during the time he was tutoring Shotoku Taishi? If so, it could have served as a model for the larger statue in wood.

Tamamushi Shrine: Jewel of Asuka Art

The Asuka period in Japan has bequeathed to the future not only sculpture of gilt bronze and wood, but also one exquisite personal

above
Closeup of the hands holding the "Wishing Jewel" on the Dream Hall Kuanyin statue. Compare with the "Little Sister" and its hand position.
below
Frontal view of the Tamamushi Shrine, Horyu-ji's Treasure Museum.

votive shrine. Empress Suiko used it herself according to tradition. The richness and intricacy precludes almost any explanation except imperial ownership. One of the most detailed and complex of all remaining Asuka works, this structure, unique in itself, combines architecture, sculpture and painting. Furthermore, it is the only remaining example of lacquer painting skills to be found in seventh-century Japan.

This wooden shrine consists of four parts — a base, a pedestal, a tiny pavilion which houses the principal image, and then the upper roof of the sanctuary. Presently it is occupied by an image of Kuanyin. (Some discussion exists as to whether or not this Kuanyin was the original occupant of the Tamamushi Shrine's sanctuary, for the inner decorations indicate that a Shakyamuni image was once intended.)

The shrine is of a size which would have enabled Suiko to keep it in her imperial quarters, there to be supplicated with offerings of rice and fruit. The royal worshipper would send her prayers upward amid the incense smoke. Asuka period devotees often called on the historical Buddha for assistance as if he were an omniscient deity rather than a great sage.

Unique Korean Bronze Masterpiece

Where the edges of the Tamamushi Shrine were joined together, they were covered with an intricate bronze openwork which shows a fully developed production technique and artistic form — not one which was part of a "makee-learnee" or on-the-job-training-program. The name *tamamushi* is originally from a beetle, whose iridescent wings were placed under the openwork bronze bands to reflect multicolored sparkles of light from the edges of the shrine. (In 1973, a Kyongju tomb excavation revealed an openwork bronze with the beetle-wing decorative technique. There are no other examples of this type of art in Japan.)

Bronze was a holy metal, for it was a combination of tin and copper, a mystical joining of elements that maintained a magical aura around the metalsmith's craft long after direct Shamanist influence disappeared. The ancient smith had been a type of shaman, transmuting raw rock through the power of fire into weapons and ornaments. When Buddhism became popular, bronze was much in demand for devotional works, for it was an unchanging metal, which aging did not attack; it resisted insects and all but the most serious fires. Furthermore, bronze could be easily plated with gold, the better for the ruling classes to display their wealth and aggrandize their name.

The gilded bronze openwork which seems to band the Tamamushi Shrine together was cut, piece by piece with a hand chisel and mallet, with obviously loving care. The designs would have been somewhat standardized at this time. The technique which had made gilt bronze saddle bow covers possible carried directly over into Buddhist art, with few changes in design or orientation. The metalsmith merely added the lotus along with the honeysuckle and quasi onion-dome, both of which were carried over from the Horserider epoch.

Elongated Figure Style

The most noticeable feature of the human figures represented on the vertical panels of the Tamamushi Shrine is their thinness, their elongation beyond the normal. This was a mannerism of the Six Dynasties in China. How did it get to the shrine which Paekche presented to Empress Suiko?

Around 550 A.D. Paekche had a very devout Buddhist as a ruler and the same phenomena was true for the Liang dynasty in China, with its capital city in Nanking.

Both kings spent a large part of their treasury on Buddhist temples and other art work, and had frequent communication with each other via ship, since from Liang boats could pass directly to Paekche without going through hostile territory.

Envoys and coasting vessels passed back and forth, as did art works and artisans. During this time the "elongated style" which was then dying out in China, may have been transferred to Paekche. Because of the disappearance of painting in this region (except for a few tomb walls), it is difficult to be certain. However, Paekche, which liked elongated curves for the drapery of its figures in bronze and in stone, would no doubt become fond of this same mannerism in the media of painting.

Since no examples of painting in lacquer presently have been excavated from the Paekche region, it is fortunate that this survives and has been carefully preserved in Japan — at Shotoku's temple of Horyu-ji. If it was sent to his aunt-empress Suiko, it would be natural that the beautiful votive shrine move to Horyu-ji upon her death in 628 A.D.

Painted Scenes

The history of lacquer painting goes back two thousand years to the Nangnang period in Korea, when China managed to gain a colonial foothold in the Taedong River basin near present-day Pyongyang. Lacquer painting was highly developed in the Nangnang area, as evidenced by Japanese excavations from 1910–1925 A.D. near present-day

above
Detail showing the Buddha hanging his cloak upon a tree branch, panel of Tamamushi Shrine, Horyu-ji's Treasure Museum.
below
A scene from the Jataka Tales of early Buddhism, illustrated on one panel of the Tamamushi Shrine, Horyu-ji.

Pyongyang. Lacquer is a very durable surface, made from the resin of a bush; lacquer resists moisture as long as temperature changes are not too abrupt. It may be termed the "world's earliest plastic."

The technique and craftsmanship which are indicated by the designs and figures on the Tamamushi Shrine point to a long-established and well developed school of art, with standardization of icons by this time. It would be difficult to claim this rapid an advance for Japan in Buddhist art, especially the difficult technique of lacquer, in such a short period of time. Earlier examples of Japanese tumuli painting indicate that when the Horseriders came to Japan, few skillful brushmasters came with them. The painting in the Flying Horse Tomb at Takehara shows how poorly Yayoi artisans could follow continental designs. The results are childlike at times during this early period. It is not reasonable to expect lacquer techniques to have sprung up in Japan like magic, without assistance from Korea, the elder brother of Japan at this time.

Korean Tigers and Garment Design

When searching for the clues to solve a murder mystery, tiny identifying marks often tell the tale, and reveal the perpetrator. The Tamamushi Shrine shows several types of "filtered" Chinese influence, although completely Korean touches can be found as well. Two side panels, which contain very rich hues even today, show touches left over from an earlier Korean period, before Buddhism. Even though limited evidence is present, one may safely say that Koguryo and Paekche line and design of a pre-Buddhist nature were close. This pre-Buddhist artistic tech-

above & below
Closeups of opposite (side) panels, illustrating the treatment of tigers and drapery, Tamamushi Shrine, Horyu-ji's Treasure Museum.

73

nique carried on for quite some time even though the story which the painting told was now Buddhist in nature.

First and foremost, tigers are not native to Japan, nor are any other of the great cats. Japanese artists never successfully represented tigers in painting until after the Hideyoshi invasion of Korea in 1592–98 A.D. The Jakata Tale (apocryphal stories about the lives of the historical Buddha) represented on one panel of the Tamamushi Shrine, shows the Buddha in an earlier life sacrificing himself to feed a starving tigress and her cubs. The powerful and properly proportioned lines indicate that the artist had an intimate knowledge of the shape and projection that a tiger should give. This precludes a native Japanese from having painted the scene. (Koreans were indeed familiar with the great cats; leopards were slain within the city of Seoul in the twentieth century, and tigers were killed in the mountains until recently.)

The stylization of the Buddha's robes in one painting had the hair fine, threadlike trailing edges seen in Koguryo painting during its Buddhist period. These trailing threads were used to portray flight and the body's aura, hallmark of a magician-shaman-holy man. The technique carries on still farther, for many Koryo-period Korean Buddhist paintings also possess this characteristic edge, now suggesting a rare and refined textile.

Little Buddhist Ambassadors

During the Asuka period many official embassies and learned monks came to the Asuka court from Korea's Three Kingdoms. Some monks remained in Japan and became naturalized; a few returned to Korea. Being men of peace and poverty, the monks could not bring gold or weapons as presents to the Japanese court of Suiko or Shotoku, but they could and did bring personal votive images of bronze.

(A)

Many gilt bronze images from the Asuka period remain in Japan, some bearing the marks of foreign manufacture. The collection of tiny Horyu-ji sculptures, numbering 52, was given *in toto* to the Imperial Household, which in turn presented it to the National Museum of Tokyo. Many of these tiny Buddhist images are Important Cultural Properties, some even National Treasures. Several of the images bear the easily discernible marks of Korean manufacture.

(A) This statuette shows an early Korean style which can be called "adapted Wei." Silla was known for its renditions of Maitreya, the Buddha-of-the-Future, for this deity had become the patron deity of the *Hwarang*, the flower knights of Silla. The crown-like protrusions seen on so many of these tiny Buddhist artifacts are a carry-over from the days of Shamanism, when the headgear was the principal part of the shamans' costume.

(B) The Shakyamuni shown here is lacking one of its attendant bodhisattvas, but shows continental influence in many respects. The one attendant figure remaining evidences Korean-style headgear (a crown) which, while not perfectly clear, shows the "climbing fire" design found in both Koguryo and Paekche tumuli from the pre-Buddhist epoch. The Northern Wei style edges of the drapery hold true to the serrated form, but the sharp-seeming edge, becomes softened without losing its regularity.

On the central figure the "Paekche brow" is noticeable. This is no more than a suggestion of a line, while the bridge of the nose sharply joins the central brow ridge. Other characteristics which label this piece "Paekche" are the opening fold of the robe on

opposite page, left, right
Three examples of petite Asuka-period bronze statuary, treasured for centuries at Horyu-ji, now in the Tokyo National Museum's Repository. All were small enough to come across in priests' sleeves.

the chest, and the softened edge of the lotus base.

(C) This gilt bronze standing bodhisattva in the repository of Horyu-ji evidences a definite, sharp-edged appearance, with a very frontal orientation, which shows not many changes from the classic Wei style. However, the headdress displays the honeysuckle design characteristic of Koguryo. The northern part of Korea has quite a harsh climate; the sharp-edged, somewhat harsh appearing statuary reveals the "hot blooded" nature of the Koguryo people. The lotus petal base shows unsoftened lines, which can be found in other works from the northern portion of

Korea, accompanied by stiffly chopped angles on the edge of the robe. Perhaps Priest Hye-cha carried this or a similar image in his sleeve when he came to instruct Shotoku Taishi in the intricacies of Buddhism?

Horyu-ji's Bronze Triad
(ht. central figure 86.4 cm.-34 in.)
(side figures 93.9 cm.-36.9 in.)

This group of figures which the Japanese call the "Shaka Triad," and rank as a great national treasure, is presently stationed in the very center-front of the dais in the Golden Hall of the reconstructed Horyu-ji. It is the largest bronze statue to survive from ancient times in the Far East. Bronze casters of China and Korea made icons this large and complex, but all have disappeared with the vicissitudes of time. Japanese scholars, realizing that no native craftsman could command such expertise in 623 A.D., are willing to see the influence of the Wei dynasty (385–582 A.D.) upon this piece. Again, sort of a "flying carpet" type of cultural transmission is visualized, even though some scholars recognize Korea as "a bridge for art from China to Japan."

Formerly, the sculptor called Tori, was admitted to have been Korean. During the colonial period in Korea, Tori's nationality was changed to Chinese. *Tol* is "stone" in Korean, and stone was the favored material for sculpture in Korea. "Tori" is the Japanized form, the "l" changing to "r." Empress Suiko ordered this Tori to cast a huge bronze image for the Soga family temple of Hoko-ji, which he did after some years of trying. One can assume that Tori was a naturalized Japanese from Korea.

According to the inscription on the rear of the "Shaka Triad" now in Horyu-ji, the sculpture was completed one year after Shotoku's death. It may have been commissioned during Shotoku's lifetime for his temple of Wakakusa-dera. After his sudden death, it was rededicated to him, for Shotoku took on the attributes of a saint after dying.

Northern Wei and Turkic Influence

In order to justify the "flying carpet" means of cultural leap-frogging over Korea, the Shaka Triad is tied closely to Northern Wei Buddhist art of China from the fourth and fifth century. The rulers of Northern Wei were not what is known as "Han Chinese." Throughout Chinese history, especially in the northern territories such as Shantung, Liaotung, and the area bordering modern Peking, various barbarian tribes (surmounting the barrier of the Great Wall of Ch'in Hsi Wang-Ti), ruled the countryside, sweeping in with the regularity of a locust plague.

The first rulers of Northern Wei could not speak Chinese at all; they were Turks, nomads from Turkestan. These Turks converted to Buddhism in the fourth century A.D. The Shamanist symbolism which these Horserider Turks had considered sacred since time immemorial was shared by the peoples of Korea's Three Kingdoms. Therefore, the jump from the Shamanist honeysuckle to the lotus of Buddhism did not take much of a mental effort; the curves were the same, only the venation and placement of the designs changed somewhat.

Crowns: Important to Horserider Descendants

The most vital part of the shamans' apparel had been his headgear, for it was the path through which the spirit flowed to heaven. This item of costume continued in importance for Buddhist art in Korea and Japan during the seventh century. The more "barbaric" designs, (those which most closely

opposite page
Shakyamuni Triad, built in memorium for Shotoku Taishi, finished in 623 A.D. Horyu-ji's Golden Hall.

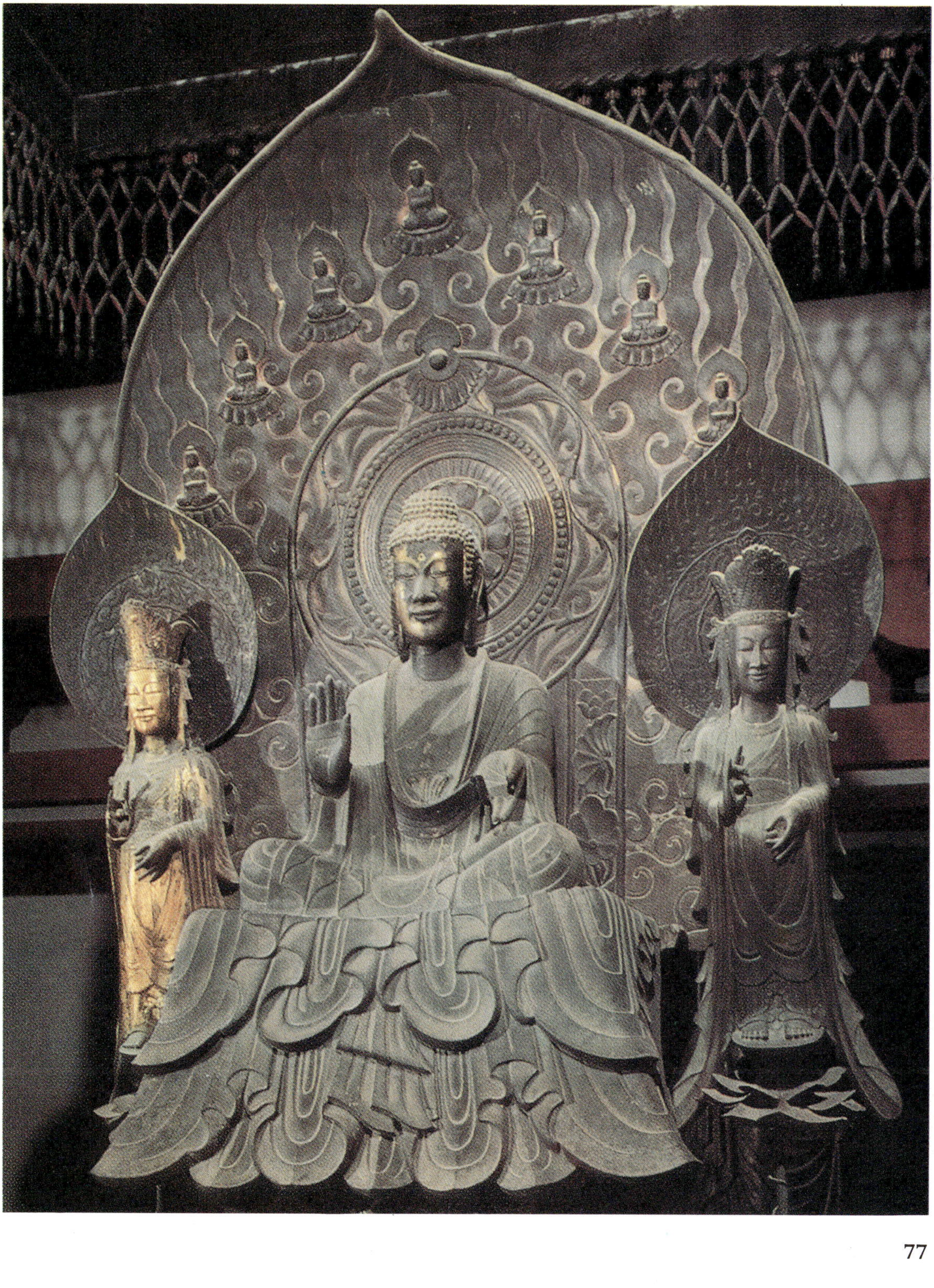

left
Kuanyin Bodhisattva, Northern Wei type, Metropolitan Museum, New York City.
above
Gilt-bronze crown (Pyongyang Museum). Note similarities to crowns of the attendant bodhisattvas.
opposite page, left
Closeup of an attendant bodhisattva (height 91 cm.) flanking the central image, Horyu-ji's Golden Hall.
opposite page, right
Detail of the brow and eyeline of the central Buddha triad, Horyu-ji's Golden Hall.

linked the Horseriders to their Shamanist past) gradually fell by the wayside.

The Northern Wei style of Buddhist art did not emphasize the importance of crowns for attendant bodhisattvas to any large extent, but due to the common Shamanist heritage of the Toba Wei and the people of the Three Kingdoms, "odd man" examples do exist. Crowns continued in both Koguryo and Paekche sharing many stylistic features. In Munyong's tomb, the king's diadem shows the same type of protrusion seen in the crowns of the two bodhisattvas attending the Shaka figure. On the right and left of the crown's centerpiece are two of the heavenward spiraling honeysuckle designs appearing throughout Koguryo and Paekche art. One might conclude that this honeysuckle leaf pattern was also copied from Wei. A single Koguryo crown remains from the Shamanist past of the northernmost of Korea's Three Kingdoms. From this pre-Buddhist artifact one can glean not only the climbing honeysuckle and fire design, but also a representation of the sun and moon, transformed into the "Flaming Jewels" of Buddhism seen on the Shaka's attendants' crowns.

The designs of the crowns which add regal bearing to the central figure's attendants were markedly different from pre-Buddhist Silla works. This is clearly demonstrated by the many objects unearthed from Silla burial mounds. Unfortunately, comparatively little has been excavated from ancient Paekche; those necropoles were often stripped by grave robbers.

The Face of the Buddha

Both the Horyu-ji Triad's central figure and those of the attendants have a sharp-edged hairline, a "vanishing" brow and the classical nose, with a bridge that has none of the shallowness found in many later Japanese Buddhist figures. The end of the nostril curve begins to flatten greatly after the Asuka period, a clear change in design as opposed to earlier Korean influences.

The faces of the Asuka-period Buddhist images were fashioned as part of the overall lost wax casting, so the finest details needed to be put in by the sculptor's chisel after the outer mold was removed. In this way, bronze was an ideal metal — easy to affix the gold-leaf covering to, and soft enough to give way to a hardened chisel without too much back-breaking effort. The eyes would be cut into the surface of the bronze, as well as nostril curve, base of the hairline, and edge of the ears. The snail curls were attached to the head of the Buddha after casting and finishing. (The snail curls on the head of Horyu-ji's central image have the same number of curves as those which have been excavated at Miruk-sa temple, built around 600 A.D. by the Paekche rulers.)

Drapery

The central figure's drapery reflects some Wei influence, but has more Korean cast than that which is "unadulterated" in the caves of Honan in north China. The outer robe has a neckline which descends in an oval shape, with a heavier protrusion (than Wei) to define the limits of the outer garment. This characteristic fold of the robe did become

79

above left
Closeup of the central Buddha's halo, Horyu-ji's Golden Hall.

below left
Koguryo-period honeysuckle and lotus design, from the ceiling of a tomb, after Buddhism accepted, 5th-6th century A.D.

above right
Rubbing showing the mandorla of the Buddha Triad, Horyu-ji's Golden Hall.

below right
Central Buddha figure showing curved mandorla, Yunkang caves, China.

popular in Sui China — but at the time of casting this Shaka image, Japanese contacts with China had been extremely limited, usually procured by the offices of coastal traders and official Korean envoys to the Sui capital of Ch'angan. The Koreans often had mixed the styles of their art inspired by China, for the "Warring States" period saw no less than six different "empires" rise and fall in north China, lasting from 386 to 587 A.D.

The Halo of the Holy One

The idea of a halo was not strange to the Horserider-Shamanist, for the Turkic-Altai stock from which the Horseriders descended used halos of a sort in their religious art. The holy aura developed quite rapidly in India after the Buddha first came to be represented in human form (circa first century A.D.). Tomb paintings of Koguryo show the first aura of Korean Shamanists as trailing streamers of fire floating upward, like the wings which are suggested by the upward-flying robes of the shamans. The large almond-shaped aura (mandorla) became popular in India before Northern Wei; it was adapted by Chinese and Koreans alike to fit their concept of how the aura of a holy man (magician) should appear.

The basic design of the halo of the Shaka in Horyu-ji's Golden Hall follows a "three-tier" pattern, with the central design being a lotus (noticeably different in design between Koguryo and Paekche). Moving outward from the center, next come radiating straight lines representing "holy light." Lotus leaves in the next circle change markedly to match with the Shamanist honeysuckle leaf pattern, while the outer portion which comes to a point at the top represents the "climbing fire" as the aura fades into the ether. It must be kept in mind that Buddhist art changed greatly in its travels across the Silk Road, even though the core remained the same, making "non-derivative" Buddhist art a meaningless term.

Within the outer tier of the Shaka's aura, which rises to a peak and curls forward (a continuation of the niche design in China's caves?) float the Buddha's seven previous incarnations. The outer aura or halo reflects the noumenal quality of the historical Buddha. The sculpturing work which delineates the hair of the tiny Buddhas (floating within the halo) indicates the Koguryo-Paekche adaptation of the snail curl for small Buddha images. This type of square-cut to represent the tightly-wound curls of the Buddha's hair is a change in stylization as Buddhist art traveled down the peninsula.

Jewelry of the Bodhisattva

The Paekche Kuanyin (Kudara Kannon) is the only image in Horyu-ji's Golden Hall which shares the adornment of both neck and wrists with the Shaka's two attendant bodhisattvas. The Four Heavenly Kings do not have a necklace, but rather a stiff collar, perhaps part of the martial nature of their accoutrements. The crown of the Paekche Kuanyin shares the same basic design of trailing pieces, while the wrists have similar bracelets; the necks of the Shaka's attendants and the Paekche Kuanyin are both encircled by necklaces. One of the more obvious links between Paekche and Asuka art is that most bodhisattvas of the two periods wear very similar jewelry. Unfortunately, no Paekche gilt bronze triads of great size remain to make an all-encompassing comparison.

The Base of the Matter

The base of the Horyu-ji Shaka shows a very complex design; few samples of Paekche Buddhist art of this period are extant for comparison. One soapstone image of the historical Buddha, located in the Seoul National Museum offers the best comparative material. From crown to base, the design of the soapstone image and that of the Horyu-ji Shaka match well — neckline curve, fold of the robe, even the drape over the pedestal at the base. Interestingly, a gilt bronze image of a bodhisattva was discovered along with the soapstone image. This gilt bronze image from Paekche has the same number of serrations in the folds of its robe. Paekche and Asuka examples show the guiding hand of a single artistic tradition.

above
Soapstone example of a solitary Paekche-period Shakyamuni statue, National Museum, Seoul.
right
One of the three canopies which hangs from the ceiling in Horyu-ji's Golden Hall.

Canopies for the Buddha: The Vault of Heaven

The *Nihongi* contains a passage stating that in 552 A.D., Paekche sent canopies and banners as a gift to the Asuka court. Canopies suggest the vaults of heaven, and three can still be seen in the ceiling of Horyu-ji's Golden Hall. The three canopies appear to be imports from Paekche, assembled upon arrival, removed during the 670 A.D. fire, and then refurbished.

The canopies were constructed of four principal segments, beveled sections fitted together with the glue after shipment. At the time the canopies were sent, several Korean masters, called *"paksa"* already resided in Japan.

Honeysuckle Leaf, Paekche Crowns and Asuka Canopies

Horyu-ji's main bronze triad is sheltered by a canopy pictured here. Decorating the upper edges are dozens of wooden angels and phoenixes carved of wood. These canopies are unique in Eastern art.

The flower designs have their nearly exact counterparts in Korea, including the number of petals, the direction of the flower's curve, and the portions which branch off. Paekche examples of this configuration did not come to light until the 1971 excavation of King Munyong's tomb in Kongju, by a team of archeologists from the Kongju Museum.

Side-by-side example of an angel and a blind phoenix from one of the canopies hanging from the ceiling of Horyu-ji's Golden Hall.

More than a dozen wooden angels were attached, separating the outthrusting edge at the top of the canopy. The complete figure of each angel is composed of three distinct parts — a backdrop of climbing blossoms and drapery, a lotus-seat, and the carved figure itself. All three pieces are incredibly detailed, demonstrating an artistic mastery of the medium.

The background piece behind each angel is wood, only millimeters thick, which precludes any type of saw being used to achieve the design. Each piece would have to have been cut bit by bit with a tiny chisel, for the soft wood would have certainly split and the entire work ruined if great care were not utilized. The blossoms and leaves of the backdrop are the climbing honeysuckle and lotus which can be faintly seen on the queen's pillow from Munyong's tomb; the designs are also seen on the gold diadems worn by the royal couple.

As for the angel figures themselves, each has the "double bun" made famous by sixth-century Sui China. All the figures have different instruments; each bears the mark of the "Paekche brow," with a high bridged nose, and a sharp cut delineating the joining of the nostril curve and lip. The eyes of the figurines seem half-closed, as in sleep, or a deep immersion in the dreamy state produced by the heavenly music from their instruments.

Blind-Flying Phoenixes

The label "blind-flying phoenix" may

above
Phoenix from Koguryo tomb mural, 4th or 5th century.
right
Design of the crown and halo for a Heavenly King, Horyu-ji's Golden Hall.

seem unusual, even for a fantastic animal, but a frontal segment of the figure's comb (much like that of a Bobwhite quail) actually is draped over the part of the head which should contain the eyes. The phoenix is one of the few fantastic animals which shares the same basic attributes in both East and West. A red bird or "firebird" was the guardian of the south, even though the origin of the design seems to be shared among more than one bird, with the physical attributes magnified.

Few examples survive of the Paekche style of depicting a phoenix, but those that do share characteristics with Koguryo. Han China showed a "three-legged crow" within the sun; this can be seen in both metalwork and painting in Koguryo. One Koguryo painting shows a phoenix pursuing another bird in the manner of a hawk; this phoenix is similar to the ones which gird the Horyu-ji canopy, but the comb doesn't droop over the eyes in the Koguryo example.

King Munyong's tomb in Kongju, dated 523 A.D., contained an artifact with the excellent but faded paintings of phoenixes on the queen's wooden headrest. At either side of the headrest were phoenix heads, carved and attached separately. All in all, the separate parts of the canopies which shelter some of the figures in the Golden Hall, carry the unmistakable stamp of transmitted Paekche art.

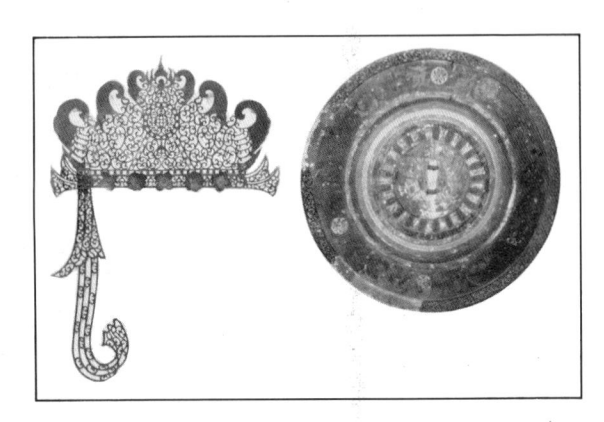

The Four Heavenly Kings

The *Nihongi* says that both Shotoku Taishi and Soga Umako promised to faithfully worship the Four Heavenly Kings if they carried the day against the Shinto ritualists in the 587 A.D. battle. The early temple dedicated to them was totally destroyed — however statues of Four Heavenly Kings from the seventh century survive at Horyu-ji. Four Heavenly Kings now present on the raised dais of Horyu-ji, stand guard on the four directions. All bear the marks of Korean influence, most notably in the crowns which rest upon the head, the shape of the faces and the cut of the clothing. Later worship of the Four Kings almost died out in Japan, while even the poorest of Korean temples displays at least four paintings, if not four huge works of sculpture representing the Four Heavenly Kings at a special entrance gate.

Gilt Bronze Openwork Crowns

The crowns of the Four Kings lacked the wrappings and protection which were afforded to the headgear of the Dream Hall Kuanyin over the centuries, so now they are in a poorer state of repair. The idea of a sepa-

Distant view of Horyu-ji's dais in the Golden Hall, showing a Heavenly King at the corner as guardian.

rate metal crown for a Buddhist deity appears to be a Korean concept. Buddhist deities in China, except for those of early Northern Wei, do not have metal crowns. The presence of crowns or elaborate headgear persisted in Korea, probably due to Shamanist influences evident in Korean Buddhism even today. Confucian Korea also emphasized headgear to a great extent.

Pinpointing the exact time when this design would have been in vogue is difficult, but the same design present on the crown of the Four Heavenly Kings of Horyu-ji can be seen throughout northern and southwestern Korea. Silla had a very different type of crown which rested upon the heads of its shaman kings.

Paekche's "onion-dome" cutouts which held the lamps in the tomb of King Munyong are used repeatedly in the crowns of Horyu-ji's Four Kings. Other designs can be seen in Koguryo painting and various remaining saddle fittings from Paekche and Kaya. The Shamanist influence can also be seen in the tiny wires which sprout in multitudinous places surrounding the cutouts in the crowns of the Four Kings. Each wire would have a tiny circular disc attached to it, mirrors to command the spirits, also to represent the sun.

Curling horns grow upwards from the edges of the crowns — their exact meaning remains a moot point. However, this is one facet of design which continued in Japan, for later headpieces of Japanese armor had "horns" which resemble those of the Horyu-ji's Four Kings very closely.

left
Closeup focusing on the drapery for one of the Four Heavenly Kings.
above
Detail showing the face and bronze crown of one of the Four Heavenly Kings, Horyu-ji's Golden Hall.

Horserider Clothing: Continuance of Tradition

The costume which drapes the figures of the Four Heavenly Kings has its sibling counterpart in Korea — the ceremonial dress of the horseback warrior — pantaloons, covered by an exterior skirt for decoration. The upper parts of each King's body are represented as though encased in the layered armor worn by warriors throughout Korea at the time, while the shoes appear to be the same as those found in tombs from Kongju to Kyongju, or seen in paintings from the Koguryo era.

Faces of the Four Kings

While most of the Buddhist sculpture of Koguryo or Paekche genesis has a distinct and unique facial set, those of the Four Kings are different. They appear less Indian than say, the figures of Shakyamuni or the Yakushi Buddha, which are also on the dais of the Golden Hall. The eyes have the same curve, and the accentuation of the base of the nostrils is very similar, but the bridge of the nose and the eyebrow line appear quite different. The Four Kings may have had a different racial background than the central Buddha figures, for the faces have Mongolian characteristics in respect to the eyes and the especially low bridge of the nose.

Were the Four Heavenly Kings modeled on the tales of "barbarian" nomadic kings (Tribes beyond the Great Wall of China were all referred to as barbarians.), who submitted to Buddhism and later became guardians of the four directions? Mahayana Buddhism,

left & right
Tapestry of Paradise, made by ladies of the court (Koreans) in memorium for Shotoku Taishi, Chugu-ji Nunnery, Horyu-ji. (Two details)

the type which finally reached Japan, was very accommodating to outside influences.

The Four Heavenly Kings in Horyu-ji, standing on the backs of four demons, do not have a terrifying mien. Later representations of the Four Kings, especially those which show Tibetan Tantric influence, are terrifying to the point of grotesqueness; this type is commonly seen in Korea today. Few representations of the Four Heavenly Kings were made after the Heian period in Japan.

A Tapestry of Paradise (623 A.D.)

After the death of Shotoku Taishi in 621 A.D., his consort commissioned three women to draw a design for an embroidery in his honor. This is traditionally held to have been a very large work, even though only fragments survive today. The type of Buddhism prevalent in Asuka at the time of Shotoku would indicate that the tapestry represented the Tushita Paradise of Maitreya, the Buddha-of-the-Future.

The clothing styles of the figures are Korean, as evidenced by near contemporary paintings preserved in Koguryo tombs. The wide-pleated skirts are seen in a more closely wrapped version adorning the Dream Hall Kuanyin, the Four Heavenly Kings, the Paekche Kuanyin, and a rock-cut image of Kuanyin found in old Paekche territory. This would not be strange, for while these works were most directly influenced by Paekche, still Koguryo and Paekche shared many things in common, such as bloodline, legal structure, Buddhist philosophy, and others.

left & right
The Buddha-of-the-Future, at Koryu-ji, ordered by Hata and put in his temple built for Korean textile workers. Koryuji's statue is recorded in 623 A.D. as an import from Korea, by the Nihongi. (Two side-by-side, entire figure and closeup of upper part)

The omnipresent honeysuckle pattern is distinct, even though the shape is more abstract than that found in sculpture. Phoenixes of the stripe which abound in Koguryo tumuli painting pass through the scenery. A seated demon wears a leopard-skin girdle as his only piece of clothing. (Leopards were unknown in Japan.) The strong Koguryo influence no doubt came from at least one of the women commissioned to draw the design, whose name was *Koma,* the Japanese word for "bear," which doubled as the name for the Kingdom of Koguryo.

The rabbit which is seen frolicking on the moon is a later adaptation of earlier beings thought to reside there. Several turtles are seen in the surviving fragments, reflecting the union of Heaven and the Sea, which had produced Ko Chumong, the founder of Koguryo.

Koryu-ji's Maitreya: Testimonial to Shotoku Taishi

The death of Shotoku saw the passing of an era in Asuka Japan, for as a statesman he possessed the rare quality of maintaining peace by the force of his personality. It is true that throughout his regency, the Soga clan leader "Horse's Child" held the final authority, but Shotoku firmly laid a base for Japanese Buddhism and also maintained harmonious relations with Silla. Keeping peace with all three kingdoms of Korea was a trick managed by few.

Among the closest associates of Shotoku Taishi was a Chinese-Korean named Hata Kawakatsu, head of a group of immigrant textile workers who worked their looms in the vicinity of what was later to become Kyoto. The Hata had made respectable contributions to increasing the wealth and prestige of Japan and had been shown special favor by Shotoku.

Hata Kawakatsu, wishing to perpetuate the memory of Shotoku, ordered a gilded figure in the shape of Maitreya (*Miruk Posal* in Korean). In the early days of Korean Buddhism, the greatest compliment was to adjudge a person to be an avatar or the Buddha-of-the-Future, who would bring final peace to earth. Apparently Hata Kawakatsu felt that Shotoku deserved that honor. Others were acclaiming him as a "saint."

A Pose of Perfect Ease

The statue seated in central position on the altar at Koryu-ji is one of the few pieces of Asuka-period art that has comparable examples existing in Korea. It is somewhat larger than its "almost twin" sitting in the National Museum of Seoul. The slight differences can be accounted for by the necessary changes an artist must make when working with bronze versus carving into wood. When the two "almost twins" were both seeable in Japan, the viewers who attended the "5,000 Years of Korean Art" exhibit, which traveled from a museum in Tokyo to Kyoto and then to Fukuoka, the close relationship to Koryu-ji's statue was obvious.

Since the wooden statue now at Koryu-ji is small enough for a trip by boat, and since the *Nihongi* itself records the arrival of a "gilded statue" in 623 A.D., which was placed at Koryu-ji, the conclusions are not hard to draw. With its original covering of gilt paint, this wooden statue looked like gilt bronze, and presumably acquired a reputation as such. Today the gilt has worn off in many places, and to some aestheticians is even more beautiful than in its original condition of the seventh century.

The two most memorable parts of this statue are the fingers almost touching the right cheek and the face itself. When compared with statues classified as "Paekche" herein, the curve of the nose and the somewhat flattened tip of the nose, as well as the sharp edge of its bridge, seem to point a finger at "Silla" in style.

Fingers and Anatomy

The fingers, which are rather abstract and too fluid in Koguryo statues and paintings, are a bit too distinctly edged in some Paekche examples. This Koryu-ji Maitreya seems to strike a balance between the two, for the digits appear both subtle yet naturally jointed, suggesting a different style.

The slender nature of the body's trunk indicates a more fully developed style than would have been seen in a Japan which had only begun to erect Buddhist temples a short generation before (Hoko-ji, for example). By the time of the creation of this statue, Silla had been officially Buddhist for about a century, and receiving influences from Chinese Buddhist art, such as Liang which did have "an elongated style."

3 KOREAN IMPACT ON JAPAN'S NARA EPOCH

Gyogi

Nara-period Japan was basically Buddhist in character. Rulers of this period turned their eyes principally towards China — even though the monks and envoys who voyaged to China usually went via the coast of Korea. Overseas travel even at this comparatively late date was still much safer when broken up into small coastal jumps. Although Buddhism was now the dominant religion in Korea and Japan, a healthy mixture of Shamanism remained in both countries' Buddhist teachings, and prophets appeared who combined the Shamanist spirits and Buddhist deities.

Gyogi, Korean in origin, is considered to be one of the prime movers behind the construction of Nara's greatest temple, Todai-ji, which housed a huge statue of Vairocana, the Cosmic Buddha. This philosophy was prevalent in Korea as well; the Korean temple of Pulguk-sa was constructed at nearly the same time. Some men seem to have been born for a certain era; Gyogi fits this classification admirably. He had a great deal of personal magnetism, and commanded a considerable following. He was even temporarily imprisoned by the Empress Gensho for the equivalent of "disturbing the peace." (Perhaps she was jealous?)

Not all of Gyogi's works were of a religious nature. He commanded the multitudes which followed the power of his voice to build bridges and roads, while a great deal of popular legend grew up around him – such as credit for the invention of the potters' wheel. (It had been brought to Japan from Korea about half a millennium before Gyogi's time.) Gyogi oversaw the erection of 49 provincial temples, and helped to reconcile the common people to the extravagance of the Nara court. It is said Gyogi collected many contributions for Nara's *Daibutsu* (Great Buddha) statue.

Gyogi's greatest religious contribution was the postulation of *Ryobu Shinto* ("Dual Shinto"). However Buddhist emperors might be, they were still aware that their "divine right" did not spring from Buddhist teaching, but rather from Shinto worship of Japan's heavenly ancestors. In a flash of insight, quite unique at that age, Gyogi made a pilgrimage to Ise Shrine, and returned, stating that Amaterasu (the primal sun-goddess) and the other Shinto deities should be regarded as avatars (previous incarnations) of the Buddha. Emperor Shomu dispatched a minister of state to question the priestess at Ise, and received a favorable oracle concerning Gyogi's manifesto. This reconciled the Shinto ritualists with the Buddhist followers, and allowed Shinto and Buddhism to accommodate each other without religious wars.

Nara's Giant Statue – Korean Success?

To celebrate the two hundredth anniversary of Buddhism being introduced to Japan by Paekche, (552 A.D.), an enormous statue was ordered. It was to be over fifty feet high and of bronze. Metals, timber and fuel were brought from all over. It required a million pounds of bronze to melt and mold it and 870 pounds of gold for the gilding! Japan was trying to emulate T'ang China in the size and splendor of her Buddhist constructions, as well as secular architecture such as palaces.

The casting began in 747 A.D. It took three years and failed six (or seven) times. The accounts vary on how many times it was not successful. To quote Professor Tsunoda:

> Six attempts ended in failure, and then the son of a Korean immigrant who had come to Japan in Tenji Tenno's time (reigned 668–671 A.D.) finally succeeded. He turned out a perfect figure of a Buddha sitting on a pedes-

above
An example of writing paper from the Nara period, stored in the Shoso-in, the storehouse for the palace furniture and the personal belongings of Emperor Shomu. This imperial storeroom established in 756 A.D., contains many objects imported from Korea.
above right
Twelfth-century painting depicting Todai-ji's huge statue of the Buddha before it was burned. Later reconstructions seem very clumsy.
below right
A tiger hunting scene reminiscent of Parhae, a breakaway northern kingdom founded in Manchuria by refugees from Koguryo after Silla unified the lower 2/3 of the Korean peninsula. The Nihongi contains several references to envoys coming from this far northern country.

tal shaped like a lotus blossom, backed by an enormous halo studded with minor statues of Buddhist saints all united in adoration, and for his remarkable achievement was honored with the fourth rank of the court.

On the death of Emperor Shomu, his devout widow willed all the furnishings of the palace to be given to Todai-ji Monastery, her husband's favorite project. These artifacts were placed in the Shoso-in, a log cabin type of storeroom, where they remained relatively undisturbed until modern times. Today one-tenth of the collection, put together in 756 A.D. on Shomu's death, is shown yearly in Nara National Museum. Each display contains annually objects of obviously Korean manufacture, suggesting the importation of fine and applied arts by the Japanese court. Today the Shosho-in is considered "the world's oldest museum." There is not space to enumerate all the works within which possibly or probably originated in Korea.

91

92

Korean Magicians and Holy Monks

Nara-period Buddhism was chiefly *Kegon* (*Hwaom* in Korean), which can be labeled as the "Flowery Splendor" sect. This Buddhist faith is perhaps the most difficult of all to follow in its endless tail-chasing perambulations; suffice to say that one did not sit cross-legged and recite a simple formula to achieve enlightenment. Of the famous Korean priests who spread the message of "Flowery Splendor," Uisang is the most noted. Uisang did not actually come to Japan, but he attracted quite a large popular following in Japanese Buddhist legend. In 1219 (?) A.D., a multi-paneled scroll called the *Kegon Emaki* was painted, (now at Kozan-ji) which documented the adventures of Uisang on his trip to China.

A lesser figure in Nara Buddhism is a Korean acolyte, with considerable magic powers. The tale is *almost* totally legendary, but that the tale itself would appear shows how respected Korean monks still were in this period. This monk kept a pet tiger, which taught him the arts of both healing and matter transmutation, by the use of a magic needle. The tiger removed the magic needle from the pillar where the Korean monk had secreted it, and disappeared forever.

This state of affairs, the loss of "a needle which could turn barren mountains green and change yellow earth to clear water," upset someone in Koguryo, whom the *Nihongi* says had the monk poisoned. Just how the tiger was brought to Japan was not mentioned. (This was about the time when the last of the important Sogas were assassinated.)

above
Section of the Kegon Emaki showing Priest Uisang and a lady who fell in love with him during his sojourn in China.

opposite page, above & below
After Uisang departed for Korea alone, the lady threw herself in the sea and became a dragon carrying his ship safely to port. Kozan-ji, Kyoto.

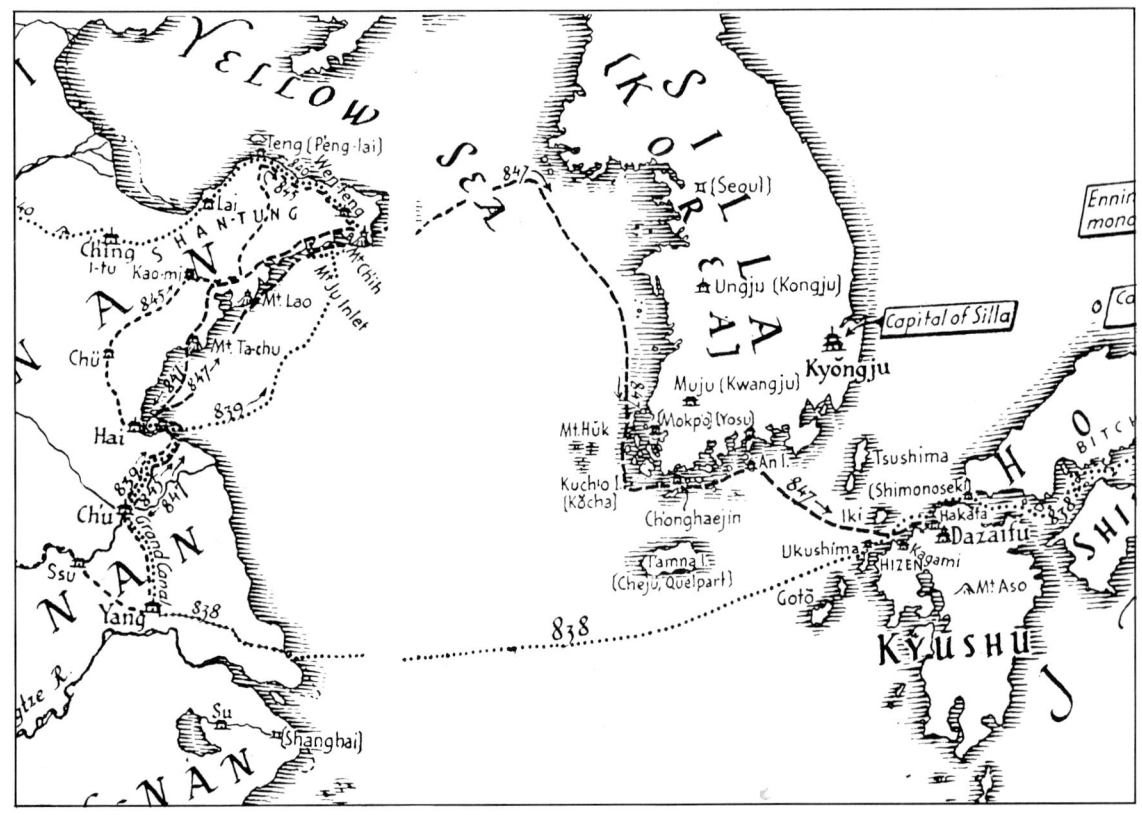

Map of Priest Ennin's travels on the ships of the Korean maritime prince Chang Pogo of Wando Island and Shantung, China.

Unofficial Transmissions of Culture

Besides the official missions, in addition to individual priests and artists who brought Korean culture to the Japanese islands, another channel existed for a number of centuries, one that is not much talked about because it reflects on the weakness of the Korean government and the greed or opportunism of Japan's seafarers. The term for these men who brought Korean artifacts to Japan, only with ideals of gain for themselves, is *wako* in Japanese and *waegu* in Korean.

At first, things were not too serious. The Koreans were better sailors and boat-builders than the Chinese, for geographical reasons. During the ninth century, a Korean, Chang Pogo, controlled a three-way trade between China, Korea and Japan because he had the most and best vessels. He claimed to have stopped "slaving" in the Yellow Sea and promoted ordinary trade. Chang Pogo built a headquarters-fortress on Wando Island, off the coast of Cholla Namdo, at the peninsula's southwesternmost tip. He also had pseudo-colonies along the opposite coast of China, with Korean wards in a big city, governed by Korean-Chinese administrators. They had temples and their own markets.

Chang Pogo's vessels carried Japanese missions to the T'ang court. As late as the ninth century, the Japanese could still not muster a blue-water fleet. Ennin Shonin, a Japanese priest who traveled to China's capital to study Buddhism, was caught during the major persecution of this religion in 845

A.D. Ennin was forced to throw himself upon the hospitality of Chang Pogo's merchantmen to gain passage home.

Especially in the Koryo period, Japanese pirates descended on the Korean coast. The worst point seems to have been reached during the reign of King U (1376–1384 A.D.) when Japanese pirate ships molested the Korean coast a total of 378 recorded times! Sometimes these later raids involved 3,000 men. The ship captains would bring not only seamen, but horses and cavalry as well as infantry. They would establish a beachhead and raid Korea as far inland as possible. In one case, the pirates reached the capital city of Kaesong. Being pirates, no loot was passed up — grains in the storehouses, horses, slaves (one raid netted over 1,000 slaves), metal weapons, paintings, silver and gold temple accessories or embroidered, gold-threaded vestments — anything not nailed down, and even some things that were!

Buddhist ritual objects were favorite targets because the altar items usually were of silver or gold and light weight. However, even heavy objects interested them. Today four Silla-period bronze temple bells and over fifty Koryo-period temple bells hang in Japan. The ingenuity of these corsairs cannot be belittled. One bell would weigh several tons. Also some paintings of Koryo period were huge. Imagine loosening a big bronze bell from its belfry, transporting it overland by sledge, loading aboard a vessel, unloading it in Japan and finding a temple as a buyer.

For smaller items, the major temples around Osaka already conducted "temple fairs" at which a miscellany of objects was sold from temporary stalls erected once a month. (Some merchants moved from temple to temple, taking their unsold items along.) This was a sort of "thieves bazaar," where the buyer asked no questions and the seller was reticent about an object's pedigree.

Due to these pirate raids, a recently unknown art form was discovered, or at least brought to public attention. The islands' most prestigious private museum, the Yamato Bunka-kan of Nara Prefecture, opened an exhibit in October, 1978, and displayed about seventy paintings which they called "Koryo Buddhist." Previously most of them had been labeled "Chinese," or "Japanese." The Yamato Bunka-kan's research uncovered about a hundred of such works of art, the majority of which seem to have come over as a result of the pirate raids. Having so many in the country may have influenced Japan's Buddhist art styles. The gold and silver sutra paintings, hurriedly acquired by the pirates, were also eagerly purchased by Japanese temples. Koreans did not use *kirikane* or cut strips of gold so much as powdered gold and "painting from the rear."

Koryo Buddhist paintings, the dozens which reached Japan while they disappeared from the Korean peninsula, present a unified style, distinct from China or Japan. (See illustration). The wire-thin lines, transparent halos, gold patterns which punctuate the robes draping the figures, do present a recognizable style — now that dozens and dozens of them have been brought together in an exhibit and catalogue.

It should be admitted, that none of these masterworks might have survived except for the activity of the energetic pirates. Japan became a well-stocked museum of medieval Korean painting. Because of the many invasions of Korea, plus the Yi-dynasty's suppression of Buddhism, few good-sized paintings survived on the peninsula from the twelfth, thirteenth, or fourteenth century.

All this activity, this "transmission of art and culture" occurred without the cooperation of either government, and, as a matter of fact, to the despair of both official sets of rulers, who could do little to control it.

"Willow Kuanyin" (Yangyu Kwanseum Posal in Korean), one of sixteen Koryo-period paintings of this exact theme presently known to survive in Japan. Most seem to have been carried there by the pirates. This example is one of three such owned by Daitoku-ji, Kyoto.

4 KOREAN INFLUENCE ON LATER JAPANESE ART

Korean Influence on the "Japanese Only" Epoch

The Heian period of Japan, lasting from 784 to 1185 A.D., has been considered free of most Chinese influences, a period during which the rulers of the insular kingdom consolidated their cultural gifts from abroad into styles which best fit the Japanese temperaments. Outside influences can still be seen in abundance though — Heian-kyo (modern Kyoto) was laid out on the plan of Ch'ang-an, capital of T'ang China. The Fujiwara counsellors saw themselves as equals of the Chinese scholar officials chosen on merit, while the truth of the matter saw breeding as the predominant factor.

The most famous novel written in Japan at this time, perhaps the most noted of all classic Japanese novels is the *Genji Monogatari*, or the "Tale of the Shining Prince." The authoress, Lady Murasaki, was an imperial lady-in-waiting, so the novel is a glamorized but basically true portrayal of the events which occurred at the Heian court at the peak of its prosperity.

The idea that the Heian period's elite culture was "strictly Japanese" breaks down very quickly in this novel of courtly romance — Prince Genji, the favorite of his father and the novel's hero, was given his name by a Korean fortuneteller! Tradition stated that the fortuneteller, who accompanied some Korean envoys, could not be received at the palace, so the reigning emperor (father of Prince Genji) went to the extreme length of visiting the fortuneteller at his residence. This would make it seem, if the Lady Murasaki were not secretly a Koreanophile, that seers from Korea were valued quite highly.

The most important occasions in the *Genji Monogatari* were celebrations and festivals at court. Here the assembled ladies and gentlemen could show off their refined breeding, especially their skills as musicians and dancers. One particular event, considered by implication to be the most important of the dance competitions, was judged by Prince Genji himself. This contest was to see which of the courtesans and grandees could best perform dances imported from the Korean court! Thus it would seem at the time of the Heian period's height, Korea had more influence than Japanese historians care to admit. There are other examples, all demonstrating that Japan may have "drawn in" on itself at the time of Heian, but it still held considerable respect for Korean culture.

Small details indicate that accessories used by the court originated in Korea also. The boudoir of Prince Genji's lady had "a carpet made of Korean brocade." Perfumes were held in high esteem; the one judged best had been a gift to Genji's father from the Korean soothsayer. The singing contest included a tune entitled "Koryo," the name for Korea of that day and age. It would appear that while Heian nobility felt pride in their own accomplishments, they still preferred Korean imports in many respects.

Impact of Official Missions on Culture

Korea and Japan exchanged a number of official emissaries; those during the fourteenth and fifteenth centuries were of particular influence on Japanese art. Zen priest-scholars were in charge of foreign affairs for the shogun, the islands' *de facto* rulers. Educated elite sat in Kyoto's officially designated "Five Mountain Monasteries" and composed poetry in Chinese (the most worthwhile occupation in their view). Thus Japanese officials welcomed and admired those Koreans with calligraphic skills.

Official embassies from Kaesong (Koryo-period capital) and from Seoul (Yi-dynasty

Korean tastes deeply influenced Heian-period music and dance as revealed in the Genji Monogatari, illustrated here. Masuda Collection, Tokyo.

capital) took care to include men excellent in ink painting and calligraphy. A custom grew up in Japan of requesting these foreign masters of ink to demonstrate their skills and leave "samples" as "presents of friendship." Farewell banquets presented good occasions for such momentoes. Often Japanese priests wrote poems of praise *(san)* above the scenes, in the manner begun by Chinese connoisseurs.

By 1450 A.D., the Japanese had come to follow this custom of decorating a painting with poetry at its top, regardless of what happened to the original composition. Korean additions tend to be more vertical; later Japanese additions became more asymmetrical.

Today Shokoku-ji in Kyoto still preserves quite a few Korean landscapes, since its priests were the most active in foreign affairs. Shokoku-ji became the home of a school of landscape painting, patronized by early Ashikaga shoguns. It dominated early fifteenth-century painting in form and technique. This so-called "Shubun School" includes many landscapes suspect of being Korean.

Tofuku-ji, another huge Kyoto monastery, also owns major Korean paintings. Furthermore it possesses Zen subjects attributed to Chinese masters (as does Japan's National

Museum). Some Western art critics suspect that certain famous "national treasures" may be later Japanese copies. But it is also possible that these famous "Chinese" paintings are Korean copies. The Koryo-period court collected a vast number of masterpieces from China. A part of each Korean artist's training entailed copying older works. All this is difficult to judge because the Korean court's collection of paintings has now vanished. In addition, no Korean temples have preserved scroll paintings older than two centuries. The Seoul National Museum's collection of ink paintings from this time is pathetically limited to less than half a dozen. Therefore, to

left
Kanzan, as rendered by Reizai, a Buddhist monk of apparently Korean extraction. Kanzan, one of the two "crazy idiots" of Zen Buddhism, is shown walking in a breeze, these feathery edges of the brushstrokes were a strong Korean technical trait.
above
Jittoku, the other of the two "crazy idiots" of Zen, by Bokkei. These two priests who were "so enlightened that they walked around laughing or chuckling night and day, convulsed at the antics of their unenlightened fellows," were among the favorite subjects of Korean monk-painters.

best study Korean accomplishments in painting during this medieval period, the serious student must turn to Japan.

Particularly after the turn of the fourteenth century, with Buddhist persecution heating

98

up in Korea, priest-artists arrived both independently and on official missions. Among the most famous names that need restudying in this regard are Kao Sonen, Reisai and Ryosen.

Towards the end the Koryo period, Korean officials were accustomed to forwarding beautiful women as tribute to the Chinese imperial court ruled by Mongols. It was but natural that they also offer their beauties to Japan's imperial court. Koryo's last mission arrived in 1391 A.D., directed to the titular emperor, imploring him to stop the pirate raids on Korea's coast. Of course this young ruler, the teenaged boy GoKomatsu, a puppet of the Ashikaga shogun, was powerless to do anything.

In 1393 A.D., a nameless favorite consort of this titular "emperor" became pregnant. Since the shogun-approved consort had not yet produced an heir, this "beautiful consort" (without a powerful native family to support her) was hustled from the palace by a *coup d'etat* to an obscure place. The baby, subsequently born on January 1, 1394 A.D., later in his poetry bemoans the cruel treatment of his mother.

This oldest child of this emperor #100, grew up as "illegitimate," to become Japan's most famous Zen priest, Ikkyu Sojun, later chief abbot of Daitoku-ji.

Among Ikkyu's best friends were several Koreans such as the painter Yi Su-mun, who left Korea in 1424 A.D., as well as this man's artist-son, Bokkei, and the artist-grandson, Jasoku. Ikkyu's memorial temple at Daitoku-ji (Shinju-an) still possesses a number of skillful scroll paintings signed by all of the four generations of artists who initiated the "Soga School." The general quality of Soga painting outrivals that of the Shogun-sponsored "Shubun School" which stemmed from Shokoku-ji. However, both obviously had some connections with Korea.

Korean Input into Japan's 15th Century Ink Painting

A number of Korea's Buddhist-oriented artists in ink, driven either by a desire to gain fame, because of their relatively greater skills, or driven by persecution in their homeland, took ships for Japan. Since then they used their Buddhist names, historical origins or birth names have been largely forgotten. Japan became their "homeland," so it is to be expected that Japanese art history now unabashedly claims these artists in ink as part of its main stream.

In a sense, these Korean refugee ink artists became Japanese. Many married native

"Wild Geese Approaching a Sandbar," by Sakan, an early 14th-century Korean painter, with an inscription by a Mongol literati I-shan, who came to Japan 1299 A.D. Ink painters and calligraphers from all three countries were very close at this time. Their nationalities later became obscured.

above
"Banana Trees in Night Rain," an ink painting with fourteen inscriptions of praise by Zen priests, apparently painted by a Korean envoy to Japan in 1410 A.D. Hinohara Collection, Tokyo.

right
One of Japan's most famous Zen paintings, attributed to Josetsu, who appears to have been a Korean refugee from Yi king's suppression of Buddhism. The painting is titled "Catching a Catfish with a Gourd," and has thirty-one poems of praise above it. Note Korean farmer's costume. Myoshin-ji, Kyoto.

women, and their children forgot their foreign inheritance, if it became convenient to do so. Many of the more famous artists of the so-called Zen school in Japan, appear suddenly, have no known birthplace or racial background, become famous, and naturally are now claimed as Japanese. Some of Japan's most famous ink painters fall into this category, names which would ring a bell among all Oriental art historians.

Rather than upsetting too many people on the basis of incomplete evidence, one example will be given here. His name is Yi Su-mun; he was born in Korea, but escaped from the persecution of Buddhism which was going on in his homeland after 1392 A.D. In 1424, while still a young man, Yi Su-mun took passage on a boat, probably the same vessel that the rather more famous and older priest-painter Shubun of Shokoku-ji traveled upon. There is an oral legend that Yi Su-mun was the son of a painter known in Japan as Josetsu, who appears out of the blue to be honored by Shogun Yoshimochi after the painter created "Catfish and Gourd."

This painting remains, owned by Myoshin-ji, and upon it is inscribed a reference to Josetsu's "new style." (Can this be a fresh breeze from Korea, coming in the 1390s?) The thirty-one Japanese priests who wrote *san* upon this "Catfish and Gourd" evidenced that they knew how to turn a phrase in literary Chinese, but not that they understood Zen philosophy.

Today Josetsu is credited as "the father of Japanese ink painting" (of the Zen-Ashikaga fashion), but perhaps he was not born and bred in Japan, as the tradition at one famous

"Full Moon and Bamboo," a segment of Yi Su-mun's "Black Bamboo Album," dated in 1424 A.D. after he left Korea. Matsudaira Collection, Tokyo.

Zen monastery avers. In any case, Josetsu soon became the darling of the Ashikaga shoguns, and was sent to acquire pillars for their new temple. Perhaps the idea had lingered that Koreans were good at architecture.

Yi Su-mun established his ability by composing an album in ink, now titled "Black Bamboo Album" and owned by Matsudaira Koto, former Ambassador to the United Nations from Japan. Ambassador Matsudaira found this series of paintings in the provinces where the Japanese name "Ri Shubun" or "The Korean Shubun" was not well known. They are signed by Yi Su-mun, and dated 1424. ("Ri Shubun" means "Yi-dynasty Shubun" or "Korean Shubun.")

For the past seven or eight decades Japanese ink painting of the fifteenth century has been dominated by three names: Josetsu, Shubun and Sesshu. Of the three, only the clear antecedents of Sesshu are known. His birth in Japan is documented, and his adult style is somewhat different from that of his teacher Shubun, whose landscapes reflect the needle sharp peaks of the Diamond Mountains of North Korea. It seems that during the half-year (1423–24) that priest Shubun of Shokoku-ji spent in Korea, he took a trip to the Diamond Mountains. Ever after that, his landscapes (or those of his disciples which are attributed to him) show such "needle points" in the background. Also, Shubun studied under Josetsu, so he may have been pre-disposed to an admiration of Korea's natural scenery.

101

left
The "needle-like peaks" so often portrayed by Shokuku-ji's Shubun school of painting. These began to appear in ink landscapes after Shubun's visit to Korea (1423–24 A.D.). Seikado Foundation, Tokyo.
above
"Vimilakirti," the famous layman of early Buddhism, part of a triptych rendered by a Korean artist named Munchong (Bunsei in Japanese) associated with the Daitoku-ji monastery's painting school. Dated 1457 A.D., Yamato Bunka-Kan, Nara Prefecture.

The important thing to note about Yi Su-mun, as an example of expatriate Korean artists of ability, is that he became the progenitor of a school of painting, the Soga School, which maintained rivalry with the court-patronized school of the Ashikaga shoguns. The landscapes painted upon *fusuma* of Shinju-an, Daitoku-ji, in 1491 by the grandson of Yi Su-mun, are the best extensive examples of ink landscape to be produced in the entire century. Furthermore, these landscapes by Soga Jasoku II remain *in situ* as sliding screen panels, so that their original use can be judged. In style, they have some mannerisms of the Sung dynasty's Ma-Hsia style, so in a way they seem less "Korean" than the famous landscapes attributed to Shokoku-ji's Shubun. It would appear that Shubun's trip of 1423–24 to Korea became a turning point in his artistic style, whereas the Korean expatriate Yi learned to accommodate his art works to current Japanese tastes. The Soga school continued as a minor influence, up until the seventeenth century. The shogunal school of painting in the sixteenth century came to reflect the new militant era of the civil wars. Art became purely patterned and innocuous in subject matter, so the artists could keep their heads on their shoulders.

Korean Tigers in Momoyama Japan

By the late fifteenth century, Japan had entered into a period entirely dominated by its military. As art patrons, the newly powerful generals wished to glorify themselves.

left
Hideyoshi, the poor boy who rose to be Japan's most powerful military figure. He sent soldiers to Korea 1592–98 A.D., but instead of conquering the peninsula and China, the principal results were a tremendous impact on the development of Japan's ceramic tradition with the importation of potters from Korea.
above
Hideyoshi's teahouse, part of his Jurakudai Palace. It now rests at Nishi Hongan-ji, Kyoto. Here he enjoyed his Korean ido bowls.

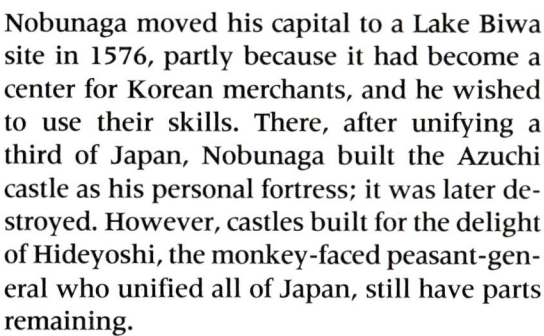

Nobunaga moved his capital to a Lake Biwa site in 1576, partly because it had become a center for Korean merchants, and he wished to use their skills. There, after unifying a third of Japan, Nobunaga built the Azuchi castle as his personal fortress; it was later destroyed. However, castles built for the delight of Hideyoshi, the monkey-faced peasant-general who unified all of Japan, still have parts remaining.

The Juraku-dai, or "Mansion of Many Pleasures," erected as Hideyoshi's main residence, served in 1587–1591 A.D., as the place where he planned his Korean campaign. Today, sections of this ostentatious building remain, reconstructed within Kyoto's Nishi Hongan-ji temple. Prominent is the tea house, and the garden Hideyoshi himself designed as a resting place to conduct the tea ceremony. This is a dry garden, filled with Sago palms, dubbed "Kokei-an," or "Tiger Glen Garden." Hideyoshi had never set eyes on a living tiger, but his returning soldiers brought back both tales and skins of Korea's most dangerous predator. The existence of Tiger Glen Garden indicates that Hideyoshi already considered himself the future master of Korea.

Both in Hideyoshi's time and later, under the Tokugawa family, painted tigers stalking through a bamboo grove with a gold-leaf background, became an oft-repeated theme. Tigers had become fashionable since the Korean invasion, while the gold served to display the ostentatious wealth of the screen's owner. Even Zen establishments, otherwise sparsely decorated, had tigers in bamboo groves as part of the temples' decor — famous compounds such as Daitoku-ji, Nanzen-ji, and several others considered it almost necessary to have at least one such painting. This may be attributed to a "Koreana" phase of

104

tradition in design. Tigers had occasionally been subjects for past Japanese painters, but the renditions were not quite right proportionally. The tigers painted in the sixteenth century, while somewhat abstract, were more realistic.

Korean Ceramics and Cultural Invasion

Only once have armed troops from Korea intentionally invaded Japan, and these were "Horseriders" originally from the extreme north; their bloodline and characteristics some present-day Koreans would not acknowledge. But Korea's ceramic tradition has "invaded" a number of times, aided and abetted by Japanese who valued the methods and aesthetics developed by its various connoisseurs, foremost of whom were its Zen-trained tea masters.

The Yayoi people who kept coming to Japan from 300 B.C. until after 300 A.D., brought to the more primitive Stone Age inhabitants such ceramic advances as the turntable first, and then the potters' wheel and the climbing kiln or "cellar kiln" *(ana-gama)*. Even the *Nihongi*, Japan's earliest official chronicles, mentions under the eighth ruler the court's sending to the early Korean colony of Izumo for a hundred potters to make funeral images *(haniwa)* of earthenware.

When the "Horseriders" erected their enormous tumuli, many thousands of ceramic images were involved. Japan's aristocratic ceramics for a thousand years was *Sueki*, a ware based in large part on that of Kaya ceramics, a type initially produced near Kimhae and the Naktong River basin in the Kaya region of Korea.

opposite page, above & below
Various fusuma or sliding wall panels, decorated with tiger paintings, a theme sparked by interest in Korea, stimulated by the war.

Tea Ceremony

It was recorded by careful tea masters that Korean-imported tea bowls or rice bowls were being appreciated and used in important ceremonies by 1537 A.D. Presumably early examples had begun to trickle in long before that. The first official tea master in Japan, Murata Shuko, may not have been able to obtain Korean ceramics easily, but it is a documented fact that his disciple Takeno Joo, praised such bowls saying, "It is no longer necessary to use Chinese wares for tea ceremony."

The simple, unpretentious, casually appearing rice bowls of Korea's late fifteenth and early sixteenth century were exactly appropriate for *wabi-cha* or "poverty-tea" as then being promulgated in the Kyoto-Sakai area. Zen's principles of understatement and frugality were expressed in clay by the provincial potters of South Korea. Of course, the Japanese have always loved to import from foreign countries, but this time they switched from Chinese bowls *(temmoku)* to Korean bowls *(punch'ong)* as being preferable.

With each year, as both the Sakai merchant tea masters and their Japanese *daimyo* patrons strove to participate in the so-called poverty aesthetic of *wabi-cha,* imported Korean ceramics came to be more and more valued. The *ido* in particular became a favorite because it had deep sides, held no special decoration, except the crackle produced in the kiln's "now moment of reality."

The peak of appreciation of Korean ceramics occurred during the decades of 1580–1600 A.D. Sen Rikyu, Hideyoshi's most famous tea master, was forced to commit suicide in 1591, but Hideyoshi continued to treasure a number of Korean tea bowls. His favorite generals in the Korean Invasion (1592–1598) surely sent back to him presents including ceramics they found that seemed suitable for the *chanoyu* ceremonies which

above
Daitoku-ji's wooden statue of Japan's most famous tea master, Sen Rikyu. (Sen is a Korean name, and he seems to be the grandson of a Korean aesthete who worked for Ashikaga Yoshimasa, and later retreated to Sakai to become a merchant.) Rikyu collected funds for erecting Daitoku-ji's Sammon (Mountain Gate) in 1588. Daitoku-ji had become the center of the tea cult. Korean folk ceramics were much admired by "poverty tea masters."

right
The interior of Ryoko-in, a subtemple of Daitoku-ji, built in 1606 A.D. to the memory of General Kuroda Nagamasa, who saw much action in the war with Korea. As a tea master Kuroda appreciated and collected Korean art, including ido rice bowls and parts of a Korean Buddhist temple.

Hideyoshi dearly loved.

A record exists that by 1572 A.D. a third of Japan's tea masters of note used Korean bowls for their tea ceremonies, but they were expensive. Sometimes the Imjin War (1592–1598 A.D.) is nicknamed "The Pottery War," because although no territory changed hands, many potters moved from Korea to Japan, either willingly or by force.

Raku Ware

Even before the war began Hideyoshi had hired two brothers, sons of a Korean-born potter, to make emerald-green decorative tiles for the roof of his pleasure palace-mansion of Juraku-dai. Under the guidance of the tea master Sen Rikyu, the half-Korean ceramists were encouraged to experiment in tea ware of the simple, unpretentious type, using Korean aesthetic values. The now-famous "*raku* ware" resulted, a low-fired ware, with thick walls, totally hand-moulded, and undecorated except for its flowing glaze, usually black or persimmon color. Kojiro, the first and most famous *raku* artist in clay, is said to have initiated tea bowls inspired by Sen Rikyu's ideals of the humble and unpretentious.

A Koryo-period granite lantern brought back by General Kuroda. It now reposes in Ryoko-in's "Reading Room Garden."

Karatsu Ware

The point of embarkation for troops bound for Korea was Karatsu. It is famous for ceramics which closely follow the Korean type. Sometimes the older pieces are called "Korean-karatsu" or *Chosen karatsu*". The earliest dated piece bears the stamp "1592." It is difficult to distinguish wares made here and on the Korean mainland, because the clay was similar with about the same iron content. An *"E-karatsu"* or "Painted Karatsu" has simple designs painted with a brush using underglaze iron, and appears very Korean in feeling.

Takatori Ware

The Takatori kilns were founded by the Korean potter Pal San; they were a simple, rustic ware similar to Karatsu. Today the kilns are near Fukuoka City, northern Kyushu. A seventeenth-generation Takatori master recently visited Korea looking for apprentices. This master-potter was one of Japan's "Living Cultural Treasures." She knew her remote ancestors were brought over to Japan during the Imjin War. (She died in 1984.)

Imari

The word "Arita" is famous throughout the world. It was on a mountainside near Arita that in 1616 A.D. the Korean potter Yi Sampyong (Ri Sampei in Japanese) discovered deposits of kaolin-rich clay suitable for porcelain production, after other Japanese had searched in vain for centuries. The area of Arita, Hizen Province, northern Kyushu, was already producing Korean-type stoneware when these deposits were discovered and production turned to porcelains. Later they were exported through Dutch ships and found their way into the mansions of Europe's elite. Imari was the seaport from which these Japanese porcelains were shipped, so "Imari ware" is also a well known expression among Western connoisseurs.

Ido

An example of the appreciation of Korean folk ceramics produced during the sixteenth century, as it was valued by later-day Japanese tea enthusiasts, lies in the history of the "Kizaimon *ido,"* a "National Treasure." Today this battered, scorched, off-center bowl, its glaze unevenly fired, is a "hidden treasure" to be seen only by the elite of teaism, after an appropriate donation. Its original, humble artisan-creator is entirely forgotten. Indeed, he is unknown, as are the craft-artists of most Korean ceramic art.

Even after the Japanese government in Edo

above
The Korean Ido, princes of Japan's ceramic "National Treasures," were originally created by anonymous Korean potters as peasant's rice bowls.
left
This is a sample of Kawai Kanjiro's ceramics, rated as Japan's number one for the twentieth century. He highly admired Korean ceramics, and was a leading exponent of Yanagi Soetsu's Folk Art Movement.

officially "closed its ports" and permitted only one ship a year at a tiny island in Nagasaki Bay, the "closed door" was still wide open when Korean vessels brought ceramics. Most were made by a special order for the Tokugawa, military dictators or supreme powers for several centuries, beginning in 1615 A.D.

Other Ceramics

General Shimizu Yoshiro of Satsuma, the extreme southeastern part of Kyushu Island, led 10,000 troops to Korea at Hideyoshi's order. He brought back at least seventeen known potters from Korea, as his "spoils of war." He settled them near his castle on Kagoshima Bay. A potter named Pak soon discovered fine clay in the hillsides, so that the Korean potters could make glazes similar to what they had produced in their homeland.

Among other famous wares begun and stimulated by Korean potters largely "kidnapped" by Hideyoshi's generals are Agano ware, produced by kilns established by the Hosokawa generals, and Hagi ware, which came out of kilns near Yamaguchi, sponsored by the Mori daimyo family. It is recorded that one potter belonging to the Hagi ware production line, its leader in fact, attempted to escape back to his native land over a dozen times, but was always caught and brought back.

The influence of Korean potters on the ceramic tradition of Japan was tremendous and has been fairly well publicized. However, the depth of this influence is unknown to most Japanese or Americans.

Twentieth Century Impact on Japanese Folk Art Movement

Japan's impact on Korea during the twentieth century is described as exploitative mercantilism by some, and in much less polite terms by others. Nevertheless, even when Korea was at its lowest ebb as a colony of Japan, influence on standards of beauty once again crossed from the peninsula to the islands.

This impetus was the Japanese Folk Art Movement, begun by Yanagi Soetsu. He lived in Korea a long time and acquired a Korean sense of artistic esthetics — the beauty of natural wood grain, the effect of bright mineral pigments, anonymity and the unselfconscious love of craftsmanship. Two of Japan's most famous folk ceramists, Hamada Shoji and Kawai Kanjiro, visited Korea with Yanagi, and picked up many inspirations from Korean "peasant art."

Some of the best pieces of Korean ceramics now in the National Museum of Korea were preserved by a friend of Yanagi, who buried them when the Korean War broke out. It may seem strange, but perhaps, among outsiders, those who most deeply appreciate Korean art, and laud it most highly, are Japanese. It is more than peculiar that the individual Japanese may rave about Korean art, while looking down on Korean people in general.

APPENDIX

To Hide History

Aside from archeology, which is restricted by the Imperial Household in Japan, the best evidence for both prehistoric and historic periods of Japan (up to the eighth century) lies in two surviving books. Their first impetus may have come from Tenchi, reckoned as emperor #39, with reign dates from 668 to 671 A.D. Tenchi was the main power in Japan from the moment in 646 A.D. when he knifed Soga Iruka, the dictator. This act ended the Soga dynasty, beginning that of the Fujiwara.

After Tenchi's death, a blood bath erupted between his brother (emperor #40) and his son (emperor #41), the former committing suicide after losing a twenty-day rebellion by his nephew. Temmu, who won the battles, realized that succession problems would plague the new dynasty if geneologies were not given official approval, and thus Japan's first written history book began. An oral court historian was summoned; events not pleasing to the ruling emperor were eliminated. However, before this volume could be finalized, Temmu died; the project remained in abeyance until a female, Tenchi's fourth daughter, ruled. She abdicated later in favor of her own daughter. The reigns of these two empresses (#43 and #44) saw the final compilation of the two basic books, the *Kojiki* (Record of Ancient Matters) and the *Nihongi* (Chronicles of Japan). The latter book was revised using a different type of Chinese spelling and is called *Nihon Shoki* (Written Chronicles of Japan). This version is easier to read, although both were written in Chinese of the T'ang dynasty or earlier styles, making it extremely difficult for anyone not a classical Chinese scholar to handle.

Western historians are fortunate that two excellent European scholars of Chinese translated these two basic books almost a century ago. The *Kojiki*, was translated by Basil Hall Chamberlain, the first recognized Western authority on ancient Japanese language. Authors of the *Kojiki* used Chinese characters for their phonetic sound rather than face meaning. Some characters were also employed for their meanings (in Chinese) and not sound. This would be analogous to using a picture of a cow and an owl to describe or render the word "cowl." Chamberlain's translation can be considered the pre-war authority. A Princeton scholar, Donald Philippi, produced a new translation, in cooperation with recent Japanese scholars. Both translations have been used by the authors, but Chamberlain's Romanization is retained and unless otherwise specified, used in the quotations.

The *Nihongi* was translated by William G. Aston, born in North Ireland; he lived and worked in Japan and Korea for twenty-five years. The large section which this book devotes to events from the sixth century through the year 697 A.D. makes it more useful when tracing the relations of Korea and Japan during the Asuka period.

Unlike the *Record*, which attempted no dates, the *Chronicles of Japan* does date events. Its chronology is unreliable until the fifth century; most events in the fourth century were placed 120 years too early, when compared with continental histories. Before the fourth century, the *Nihongi*'s dates are not reliable at all. For example, Japan's first dozen emperors are given an average of over a century of life, when the lifespan for Japanese a millennium later was about twenty-seven.

Slanting the Books

When the *Record of Ancient Matters* and the *Chronicles of Japan* were compiled, Japan had recently been swelled with refugees from Koguryo and Paekche. These "boat people" were the intellectual cream of the two kingdoms, which had been conquered by Silla (with the help of the T'ang Chinese army). Korean-descended rulers no longer sat in the catbird seat of power in Japan, but the influence of Koreans was still considerable. Because of their gifts of civilization, high places were occupied by Koreans and also Chinese who had often first lived in Korea for a generation or so.

Silla had been the refugees' historic enemy. Scholars from Paekche, because their classical Chinese was superior, helped to collate the two historical works, particularly the *Nihongi*. They had opportunities to cast a bad light upon Silla. This included claiming that Silla had been under the control of Japan for more than a century. The text was "slanted" accordingly.

Actually writers living in the early eighth century did not have too clear a picture of events during the fourth century. They seem to have used ancient Korean or Chinese historical role-models whenever possible, stealing rulers from ancient continental history, filing off the serial numbers so to speak, then inserting these "emperors" into embarrassing vacancies. Confucian-style motivations credited to some of the early rulers also reveal borrowing from the continent.

Legitimizing a New Dynasty

The primary purpose of these two history books was to give the new Fujiwara dynasty a credible family tree. The idea of "imperial authority" or "one unbroken line for ages eternal" was still in its infancy. However, those who wrote for the new dynasty nationalized the Horseriders (such as converting Jingu into a Japanese) and thus obligingly traced Fujiwara-dynasty rulers back to the Sun Goddess. However, either through oversight or intentionally, the Paekche authors did leave in some revealing "clues," which added together and put under careful scrutiny reveal a great deal about actual events.

Tool in the Hands of Empire Builders

The grandiose claims in these two early history books, giving an "Imperial Descent from the Sun Goddess" to the existing rulers proved very useful to a group of militarists at the time of the Tokugawa shoguns' overthrow. They had ruled Japan for almost three centuries, relegating the emperors to a cloistered or honorary existence without power.

With the coming of Commodore Perry's black ships, Japan was given a rude awakening; it seemed to be far behind the Western powers in military might. When the Tokugawa shoguns were demoted, the new military powers, the Sat-Cho clans, saw that colonial expansion was the name of the game in the late nineteenth century. Either Japan must catch up, or it might become a quasi-colony itself.

One prime mover in using the two ancient books to unify the fragmented Japanese *vox populi* was a statesman named Ito Hirobumi. In order to make Japan strong, he needed nominal but absolute control; the figurehead ruler became a living god, but one controlled by "advisers." Since the early Japanese history books traced the ruler's descent from the Sun Goddess, the figurehead could be made to look "infallible," even more convincingly than the pope had become the infallible ruler of the Roman Catholic church.

State Shinto was promulgated, with the emperor as its head. The ashes of those who died in efforts to expand the empire went to Yasukuni Shrine to be deified. A small military and industrial elite controlled Japan by the 1920s.

Korea became the first Japanese colony. Korea's role in civilizing the islands was conveniently buried; now that more than a generation has passed since the colonial stigma was removed, it is time to look in the closet and recognize the cultural-familial relationship of these two countries.

ABRIDGED BIBLIOGRAPHY

Akiyama, Terukazu and Matsubara, Saburo, *Arts of China: Buddhist Cave Temples—New Researches,* (translated by Alexander Soper), Tokyo and Palo Alto: Kodansha International Ltd., 1969.

Anesaki, Mashaharu, *Religious Life of the Japanese People,* Tokyo: Kokusai Bunka Shinkokai, 1970. (reprint)

Blacker, Carmen, *The Catalpa Bow: A Study of Shamanistic Practices in Japan,* London: George Allen and Unwin Ltd., 1975.

Brinkley, F., *A History of the Japanese People,* New York and London: Encyclopedia Britannica, 1913.

Chamberlain, Basil Hall, *Things Japanese,* Yokohama: Kelly and Walsh Ltd., 1891.

Cole, Wendell, *Kyoto in the Momoyama Period,* Norman: University of Oklahoma Press, 1967.

Dilts, Marion May, *The Pageant of Japanese History.* New York: Longmans, Green and Co., 1938.

Eckart, Andreas, *A History of Korean Art,* (translated by J.M. Kinsley and M.A. Oxon), London and Leipzig: Edward Goldston and Karl W. Hiersemann, 1929.

Egami, Namio, *The Beginnings of Japanese Art,* Tokyo: Weatherhill-Heibonsha, 1969.

Gale, James Scarth (revised by Richard Rutt), *A History of the Korean People,* Seoul: Royal Asiatic Society, Korea Branch, 1972.

Gorham, Hazel H., *Japanese and Oriental Ceramics,* Tokyo and Rutland: Charles E. Tuttle Co. Inc., 1971.

Griffis, William E., *Corea: The Hermit Nation,* New York: Charles Scribner's Sons, 1882.

Ha, Tae Hung, *Tales from the Three Kingdoms,* Seoul: Yonsei University Press, 1970.

Han, Woo Keun, *The History of Korea,* (translated by Lee Kyung Shik and Grafton Mintz), Honolulu: University of Hawaii Press, 1974.

Harada, Jiro, *Japanese Art and Ideals,* Tokyo: Kokusai Bunka Shinkokai, 1937.

Henthorn, William E., *A History of Korea,* New York: The Free Press, 1971.

Hulbert, Homer B. (ed. C.N. Weems), *History of Korea,* (two vols.), New York: Hillary House Publisher Ltd., 1962. (revised reprint)

Ilyon, *Samguk Yusa,* (translated by Ha Tae Hung and Grafton Mintz), Seoul: Yonsei University Press, 1973.

Joe, Wanne J., *Traditional Korea: A Cultural History,* Seoul: Chungang University Press, 1973.

Kidder, Edward J., *Masterpieces of Japanese Sculpture,* Tokyo and Rutland: Bijitsu Shuppansha and Charles E. Tuttle Co. Inc., 1961.

_____, *Japan Before Buddhism,* New York and Washington, D.C.: Frederick A. Praeger Inc., Publishers, 1959.

Kim, Hong Hak, *The Prehistory of Korea,* (translated by Richard and Kazue Pearson), Honolulu: University of Hawaii Press, 1970.

Kim, John (ed.), *Korean Art Seen Through Museums,* Seoul: Eastern Media, 1979.

Kuck, Loraine, *The World of the Japanese Garden: From Chinese Origins to Modern Landscape Art,* New York and Tokyo: Walker-Weatherhill, 1968.

Kuno, Takeshi and Suzuki, Kakiji, *The Art of Japan: Horyu-ji,* (Horyu-ji) Tokyo: Shogakkwan Co. Ltd., 1966.

Lee, Sherman E., *A History of Far Eastern Art,* Edgewood Cliffs and New York: Prentice-Hall Inc. and Harry N. Abrams Inc., 1973.

Lee, Tong Ju, *Korean Paintings in Japan, (Ilbon sok ui Han Hwa),* Seoul: Somundang, 1973.

_____, *Koryo Buddhist Paintings, (Koryo Bul Hwa),* Seoul: Chung Ang Ilbo, 1982.

Mizuno, Seiichi, *Asuka Buddhist Art: Horyu-ji,*

(translated by Richard L. Gage), New York and Tokyo: Weatherhill-Heibonsha, 1974.

Murasaki, Shikibu, *The Tale of Genji,* (translated by Arthur Waley), New York: Random House, 1960.

Murdoch, James, *A History of Japan,* (two vols.), London: Kegan Paul, Trench, Trubner and Co. Ltd., 1925.

Noma Seiroku, *The Arts of Japan: Ancient and Medieval,* (translated by John Rosenfield), Tokyo: Kodansha International Ltd., 1965.

Ooka Minoru, *Temples of Nara and Their Art,* (translated by Dennis Lishka), New York and Tokyo: Weatherhill-Heibonsha, 1974.

Papinot, E., *A Historical and Geographical Dictionary of Japan,* Tokyo: Charles E. Tuttle Co. Inc., 1972. (reprint)

Posonby-Fane, Richard A., *Imperial Cities: The Capitals of Japan from Oldest Times until 1229,* (compiled by Michael Moscato) Washington, D.C.: University Publications of America Inc., 1979. (reprint)

Reischauer, Edwin O., *Ennin's Travels in T'ang China,* New York: The Ronald Press Co., 1955.

Reischauer, Robert Karl and Jean, *Early Japanese History,* (two vols.) Princeton: Princeton University Press, 1937.

Saito, Tadashi and Itsuji, Yeshikawa, *The Art of Japan: Prehistoric Art, (Keshi Bijitsu),* Tokyo: Shogakkwan Co. Ltd., 1970.

Sanders, Herbert H., *The World of Japanese Ceramics,* Tokyo and Palo Alto: Kodansha International Ltd., 1967.

Sansom, George, *A History of Japan to 1334,* Stanford: Stanford University Press, 1958.

Sohn Pow Key; Kim Choi Chun; and Hong I Sun, *The History of Korea,* Seoul: The Korea National Commission for UNESCO, 1970.

Spieser, Werner, *The Art of China,* (translated by George Lawrence), Baden-Baden: Crown Publishers Inc., 1960.

Willets, William, *Foundations of Chinese Art: From Neolithic Pottery to Modern Architecture,* New York; Toronto; and London: McGraw-Hill Book Co., 1965.

Yasumaru, Futo no Ason, *Kojiki,* (translated by Basil Hall Chamberlain), Tokyo: Charles E. Tuttle Co. Inc., 1982. (reprint)

_____, *Kojiki,* (translated by Donald L. Philippi), Tokyo: University of Tokyo Press, 1968.

_____, (ed.), *Nihongi,* (translated by W.G. Aston), Charles E. Tuttle Co. Inc., 1972. (reprint)

Catalogs

Kyoto National Museum, "Takamatsu Tomb," National Treasure Series, Kyoto: n.d.

Nara Yamato Bunkakan Museum, "Korean Buddhist Paintings of the Koryo Dynasty," Nara: Yamato Bunkakan Press, 1978.

Osaka Municipal Museum, "Japanese and Korean Cultural Transmissions, "Tokyo: 1980.

Puyo National Museum, "Puyo National Museum," Seoul: Samwha Publishing, 1977.

Periodicals

Chon, Kwan U. "A New Interpretation of the Problems of Mimana," KOREA JOURNAL, Seoul: Feb. & Apr., 1974.

Covell, Jon Carter, "Korea's 'Gifts' to Japan in the 6th Century," MORNING CALM, Seoul, Dec. 1983.

Covell, Jon Carter, "Korea's Unknown Legacy from the Koryo Period" KOREA JOURNAL, Seoul: Dec. 1978.

Ishida Eiichiro, "A Treatise on Japanese Culture," CHIKUMA SHOBA, Tokyo: 1969.

Li, Ogg, "On Accounts of the Wei-chi Tung-i-chuan," THE FIRST INTERNATIONAL CONFERENCE ON KOREAN STUDIES, PAPERS, Seoul: December, 1979.

Ledyard, Gari, "Galloping Along with the

Horseriders: Looking for the Founders of Japan," JOURNAL OF JAPANESE STUDIES, Tokyo: Spring, 1975.

_____, "How the Linguist's Tail is Wagging the Historian's Dog," Seoul: KOREAN STUDIES FORUM, Spring, 1979.

McCallum, Donald F., "Korean Influence on Early Japanese Buddhist Sculpture," KOREAN CULTURE, Vol. 3, No. 1, March, 1982, Los Angeles.

猛虎牙説散逢愁土東海
政危横行者誰識人中公
同
甲午南善